THE IGNOBLE PARADOX OF MAN

I0420079

by
Brian C. McGuire
Towson University

FAR-LEFT PUBLICATIONS

The Ignoble Paradox of Man

The Ignoble Paradox of Man
Copyright 2019 - Brian C. McGuire
Library of Congress 1-2517615671

ISBN: 13:978-1518835957
ISBN: 10:1518835953

Printed in the United States of America
10 9 8 7 6 5 4 3 2

Brian C. McGuire

The Ignoble Paradox of Man

Brian C. McGuire received a Bachelor of Science from Towson University. His areas of research interests include the mental terrain of Community Psychology: A field of Human Services that places special emphasis on problems associated with urban groups and how they adapt under low socioeconomic conditions during childhood, adolescence, and throughout the course of adult development and aging, and sociocultural influences (including theoretical concepts pertaining to how various dimensions of culture influence stress and coping).

Dedication

To my people and all Americans in the struggle: Raising social awareness and increasing cultural literacy will boost low self-concept and esteem. For it is through our undifferentiated consciousness we learn how to overcome the shackles of mental colonialism—a racial policy in which the oligarchy seeks to control a nation often for their own benefit while exploiting, oppressing, or humiliating its minority members.

The Ignoble Paradox of Man

TABLE OF CONTENTS

Prologue: On the Ignoble Origins of Paradoxes

Introduction: The Ignoble Paradox of Man

The Concept of Racial Inequality
in Conservative White America
Chapter 1

Language of the Unheard:
The Baltimore Riots of 2015
Chapter 2

Biracialism in America
Chapter 3

The Plight and Predicament
of Blacks in America
Chapter 4

Several Key Issues Affecting Blacks
and their Support for Homosexual Rights
Chapter 5

In the Age of Trumpism:
A Backlash of Hostility
Chapter 6

Black Morality: A Taboo Topic
among White Americans
Chapter 7

Epilogue: Diversity and Divergence

Prologue
On the Ignoble Origins of Paradoxes

Dale Berra, son of the New York baseball hall of famer Yogi, was once asked to compare himself with his famous father. He said, "We are a lot alike, only our similarities are different."

James M. Jones,
Prejudice and Racism (1971-1995)

I began to write <u>The Ignoble Paradox of Man</u> on January 10, 2012, amid the faculty of indiscretions concerning race, ethnicity, and culture. It is going to sound like a personal fable when I tell you the book started out as an essay I wrote over twenty years ago. I spent a considerable amount of time, since then, devoted to understanding paradoxes. So, I always wanted to work with the title again. This time, I have enhanced my experiences as a father, former soldier, and college scholar to use as I embark upon this project. However, I am now concerned about discussing paradoxes as the focus of public discourse. Having a strong psychology background, any attempts at writing could emerge to form a more encompassing representation of the discipline.

Certainly, I am corrupted by my ignorance and passion for classic psychology since most of what I now write I learned from classically trained psychologists. On the one hand, psychologists continue to embrace open discourse on the human psyche, a broadening that makes Western civilizations like the United States a democracy. Yet, as a science, psychology is the province of a single culture (American) and a single social class (middle). The lack of minority topics in the field makes for rare and short-lived moments people will work to improve the lives of one another. Indeed, psychology is a middle-class, White American male profession. In this way, I am preoccupied by the domain of information obtained from my oppressors.

Perhaps, you would be greatly dismayed or even horrified to know psychology has always played a vital role in racism and racial discrimination. Wilhelm Wundt (1832-1920), James B. Watson (1878-1958), and B.F. Skinner (1904-1990), each held supremacy beliefs about the inferiority of Blacks, Jews, and those considered unacceptable. The Russian Ivan Pavlov (1849-1936) published his results of learning experiments with dogs. He would soon begin to experiment on Jewish children in one of the most cruel, genocidal experimentations involving ethnic-cleansing. His practice is known today as classical conditioning. Even Arthur Jensen, who writes popular theories about racial intelligence, condemning African Americans, contributed a legacy of ideas to racism and racial discrimination. Then there was Dr. Benjamin Rush— an American medical physician whose face has since 1965, served as the official seal for the American Psychiatric Association—who contributed to racism and racial discrimination through the eugenics movement. I find these theorists most fascinating.

On the other hand, I continue to recognize the dearth of minority professionals in the field. The lack of competing cultural groups—Blacks, Latinos, Native Americans (American Indians), females, people of different cultures, individuals from low socioeconomic backgrounds, and other minorities, both student and professional, reinforce the understanding minorities—have needs that are not being met today.

However, the American Psychological Association is once again recognizing minority issues as a mainstream topic in the field. Thanks to scholars like Stokely Carmichael and political scientist Charles Hamilton who coined the term *"institutionalized racism"* in the 1960's, and social psychologists like James M. Jones (1971-1995) who gave us a three part definition for racism, psychology reexamined its basic principles and own relevance as a science profession. Also, kudos to pioneering research conducted by psychologist George Sanchez, a Hispanic male who demonstrated intelligence tests are culturally biased against minority children. Their important contributions paved the way for me to write on topics like The Ignoble Paradox of Man as a psychology and concern.

The Ignoble Paradox of Man can teach people to think of absurdities existing between the larger society and smaller cultural groups as paradoxes. Paradoxes call to attention the moral and intellectual advancement of culture or why humanity inevitably reflects base motives. For instance, the vile development of slavery, the system of segregation, and the eugenics movement were all ignoble efforts to advance American culture. The claim these practices were marked by concern, motivated primarily with the alleviation of suffering, in the contexts of sociocultural discourse, directly contradicts human decency.

Today, the circumstances of American culture are far more forgiving than in past times. Although, occasional incidents of human indecency continues to spark conflict and hatred in ways that reflect base motives. Thus, an ignoble paradox continues to cause great suffering among Blacks and other minorities.

Certainly, paradoxes are not new; nor are existing paradoxes simply and certainly, in any way, gone. Not much has changed in the new millennium, either. Unprincipled criticisms about minorities continue to raise dialogue around human decency. In this way, awareness for the persistence of White resistance remains strong. For the above reasons, we have become a nation of opposites, hence, the reason for writing this book.

What's ignoble about human motives that would cause a paradox? First, an *ignoble motive* describes how a person's gallantry can be misguided, particularly when people needs have gone unmet. For instance, Rodney Solomon and Bernard Miller were convicted in 1993 for the death of a thirty-four year old woman. She was dragged one and a half miles during a carjacking. What could possibly be gallant about this story?

Apparently, the two men were trying to return a teenager home to her parents in New York from Washington, DC after she was kidnapped and taken across several states by her much older boyfriend. However, the two men were misguided in thinking a carjacking would function as a successful avenue to end their problems. Yet, they were noble in their efforts to extend a courtesy to the young girl in distress. Curiously, both men chose not to take the girl to the proper authorities. In this case, they had fearful expectations of police. Ironically, Mrs. Pam Basu, the carjacking victim, died while her baby rested in the back seat of her stolen car.

Now that we know what's ignoble about human motives, just in comparison, what's a paradox? A *paradox* appears to be a self-contradiction. A classic example of a paradox is the statement, "I lie all the time." If a person lies all of the time, then how can anyone tell when he or she is being truthful or deceitful? In this case, the statement appears to contradict itself.

The fact that Rodney and Bernard also feared law enforcement in which officers are sworn to protect civilians is a paradox. Their ambivalence about seeking help from authorities describe the conflict Black Americans experience between their moral values and negative feelings they have for a nation considered hostile.

What's ignoble about their story is that the twosome committed a gruesome carjacking in the name of gallantry. In this way, an ignoble paradox is born. Their motives were noble, yet misguided. And, their actions seemed to contradict human decency. As you can see, paradoxes appear contradicting but, nonetheless, are possibly true.

Paradoxes can cause people to oppose one another. The United States existing in continuous recessions often creates competition among people. In this time of national distress, a declining economy may cause great divergence among different groups of people. In turn, governments will place greater value on the dominant culture. For instance, President Obama promised to restore the middle-class while numbers for the poor increased.

Ironically, people will unite for the greater purpose of common good. But, in the United States and other Western cultures, it is no coincidence recessions come at a time when governments expand militaries, militarize actions abroad, or reorganize and reconsolidate its resources. The fact is governments lie all the time about the current state of affairs, which means certain paradoxes draw from enormous human consequences.

As you can see, paradoxes make for great psychological discussion. Today, however, I have broaden my discussion to include open discourse on cultural problems and the estranged politics of Republicanism, an ideology gone terribly wrong, one in which its supporters stubbornly refuse to make compromises and concessions. Also, the Democratic Party does not go without scrutiny for their mishandling of intergroup relations.

Democrats (liberals) are guilt ridden by the presence of Blacks in America. They're so guilt ridden most of them are unable to put minority problems and concerns out their consciousness. In the course of freeing themselves from guilt—through remedial programs and Affirmative Action policies that support minority mobility—they may simply fail in their efforts to allow Blacks the right to deviate from accepted standards of American democracy.

In their quest to include and integrate Black Americans into mainstream culture, liberals may inadvertently cost them the right to follow their own ambitions. In this way, liberals fail to allow Blacks to bring a different set of talents into consideration. Their natural abilities could reverse their situation of disadvantaged so it becomes advantageous to them.

In the past, Blacks and Puerto Ricans were denied access to important opportunities like rights to public office and access to public accommodations: fair housing, restaurants, et cetera. Today, conservatives continue to resist programs that would help minorities achieve opportunities. Affirmative Action and school desegregation are two such examples. These exclusionary processes, described as humiliating, emasculating, and degrading, not only to Black and Puerto Rican youth, but most ordinary people living in America as United States citizens, caused minorities to suffer indignity.

The thuggish mentality they adopt from social indignity leads many to find alternative lifestyles. Drug dealing, prostitution, and other criminal related activities are alternative lifestyles that often results from being disadvantaged or having a lack of opportunities. Despite their feelings of indignity, some minorities, particularly Blacks and Puerto Ricans, learn to benefit from alternative education and other opportunities.

Alternative education and other opportunities would change the attitudes of Blacks in the coming generation. Unlike the sixties, the first time Blacks attempted to overcome, the millennium's dawn would unveil new opportunities, forever changing the sociopolitical climate of culture. It was here, poor Black and Hispanic Americans would change the attitudes of Whites in the coming generation.

Blacks began to mainstream their issues and concerns, slowly penetrating the larger society. Although they experienced strong resistance from conservative Whites, economic decline in employment wages, and a wide spread gap between middle and upper classes in ways that affected generations of working class poor, Blacks gave birth to an affinity; and, its impact is undeniable.

The emergence of Hip Hop was an undeniable legacy of great consciousness for both Black and Hispanic youth. It was a time in which they would unite to uplift themselves, changing the thinking strategies of mainstream, homogenized Americans. This moment in history showed people just what happens when minorities follow their own ambitions.

Not so long after Blacks overcame the mental shackles of racial segregation (1809-1967), violent attacks against African and Hispanic American students forced Kevin Donovan to end mainstream abuse of minorities. Donovan, an African American DJ from South Bronx, New York, formed a treaty with Latino gang members.

Many parented children who attended school at historically White educational institutions like Christopher Columbus High School in the North Bronx. His efforts resulted in a style of popular music originating from US

Black and Hispanic Americans, featuring rap with an electronic backing. The result was break-dancing.

People like Kevin Donovan (now Afrika Bambaataa), Latinos, and other minorities would again be met with resistance and guidelines for social acceptance, which worsened intergroup relations. They found themselves under investigation by federal, state, and local agencies. Such intense investigations took place because of an alleged conspiracy to forcibly overthrow existing powers of authority.

Break-dancers, known for dancing on street corners, now faced possible prosecution for having social gatherings and making rhythmic movements that mimicked Caporaria, a Brazilian combat art. Many break-dancers living in minority segments were subject to a particular process of violent physical treatment and psychological conditioning that should have left them lethargic. But, lethargy never entered into their new conscious representation.

Conservatives lobbied against this cultural juggernaut, but soon found out minorities in the coming generation would bare their own identity. Unfortunately, after years of lobbying, break-dancing was finally outlawed on big city street corners. And, legislation proposed that such an art form, if it is in fact a dance, should only be performed in nightclubs.

Sociocultural psychologists and experts adept at understanding the intimacies of intergroup behavior believe legislation against break-dancing was an attempt to destroy a unity that encouraged racial integration. Still, thanks in part to their latest contribution, people from all walks of life openly embrace Hip Hop culture. Many openly cross racial boundaries despite the persistence of negative media imagery. For in the face of adversity, Hip Hop showed their natural abilities to develop into more than what the future holds for them.

There exists a cultural divergence from which people are regarded as having separate experiences. Such a culture of divide is critical to whether we, as a nation, can move forward beyond our likes and dislikes long enough to keep alive the hope of America democracy. Yet, America is a country preoccupied with hopes and dreams.

Still, another cultural limitation is a decrease in trust. The lack of trust removes from possibility complete confidence in the American people. The US Government has built a culture of fear on racist assumptions. Fear is so prevalent it has digressed into aversions that reinforce social separation. This ignoble paradox begs the question, "For whom and under what set of circumstances is the American dream possible?"

For whom and under what set of circumstances can people partake in the American dream? A stronger understanding of the American dream evolves the enslavement or dispossession of Black people. Throughout their intellectual history, White Americans excluded and persecuted Black people, world cultures even. This type of oppression is the America we all have come to know. Such a time of oppression and degradation should, in fact, be part of America's past. However, there is something ignoble about this moral reasoning.

Racial oppression is based on the principles of American democracy. In this way, how can a people who were excluded and persecuted under the very principles from which freedom rings become a part of the American dream? The changing demographic tapestry of American culture promises greater national diversity. It also carries the challenge of extending the American dream to people it oppressed. For today's Whites to embrace a much more accepting attitude toward minorities, without recognizing those facts, greatly contributes to the plight of Blacks and furthers minority predicaments.

In this way, paradoxes continue to cause divergence between the larger society and smaller cultural groups in America. Understanding that the larger society may experience conflict between their genuinely egalitarian values and own negative feelings toward Black Americans cause Whites to feel discomfort, uneasiness, and fear. Such ambivalence brings forth a number of important issues.

In contrast, people expect to see the nation come together on a number of key issues. In Chapter 5, several key issues affecting Blacks and their support for homosexual rights are discussed. It was said Black people came together with conservatives in 2008 to vote against proposition 108—a ballet enabling people to marry persons of the same-sex. In order to create positive change in current thinking strategies, lesbian, gay, bisexual, and transgendered individuals (LGBT groups) recently united in good sense. That is, LGBT groups joined other minorities in a common purpose.

As concluded in Chapter 5, positive change for LGBT groups depend on the state of relations between these two cultural systems. The merging of civil and LGBT rights groups ensured this unity. In this way, readers will gain a new understanding for complications found to exist between the larger society and smaller cultural groups. Paradoxes existing in this book reflect real beliefs about community and wellness. Thus, minority issues should loom large with readers by the end.

Readers will also learn how paradoxes work with sociocultural influences to penetrate the human psyche. Paradoxes can arouse both the emotional and mental anguish of prejudice and hate. Certainly, had it not been for the tragic events surrounding Matthew Wayne Shepard—a White male homosexual and student at the University of Wyoming, who died from a gay bashing, and James Byrd, Jr., who was dragged to death down a three mile stretch of country road simply because he was Black—African Americans might have become less suspecting of people like George Zimmerman and his cries of victimization in the Trayvon Martin case.

What's ignoble about this paradox is how dominant White Americans withdrew their concerns for Trayvon once they found out he was a young Black male. Zimmerman, on the other hand, received overwhelming financial assistance from White supporters in what was said to be an act of good faith. Zimmerman, a White and

Hispanic biracial male, appealed his innocence to the public. In this way, paradoxes show how society can quickly focus on important issues, only to withdraw from active participation due to intergroup differences.

White Americans have an elaborate system of dealing with minorities, which must be balanced to reach full equality. Whites are consumed by their ignorance and love of Western civilization. So, unless they are socially aware and culturally literate, many will have a poor perception of minorities.

Curiously, conservative White Americans tend to resist modern change. Why so? It puts forth realistic responses to progress and reform. Thus, when real change is present, conservative Whites will separate themselves from society, and at the risk of excluding minorities. Have we not yet learned anything from cultural problems that disadvantage the country?

Resistance is shown by conservative supporters through their discomfort, uneasiness, and fear of change. In contrast, America's changing tapestry reflects a society in which people are apparently working to correct these cultural discrepancies. Corrections are being made even though opposing factions continue to show resistance. That conservative people fear change often plays an enormous role in whether White Americans will become more sensitive to the psychology of issues and concerns for minorities. Incidentally Blacks, made to endure past oppression, are still excluded from obtaining the American dream and in pursuit of their own happiness. Such an oppression of people undermines American democracy to the point that taking part in the American dream becomes a cliché.

The vast majority of Whites ostensibly support minorities in their quest for the American dream. However, we must remember that up until recently, most discriminated against minorities from all walks of life. In this way, it may be too early to conclude whether conservative White society will continue to move steadily forward toward liberal racial attitudes. Or, will it become listless and inactive in its resistance toward further change.

For now, comments about freedom and democracy for all sound a bit vacuous. In other words, White people always claim minorities have the right to partake in the American dream. But, behind closed doors, many continue to discriminate. In that way, their support for general principles of equality is espoused in the abstract.

Why do minorities continue to embrace Western society? What makes America a democracy for minorities today? It is not only a political system governed by people or their representatives, but the possibility to succeed in society because of existing opportunities made available by new circumstances never before in their favor.

In the new millennium, social separation characterizes mainstream society. In this case, its apparent support for American democracy may be superficial. This observation comes at a time when minorities are beginning to wield more political power.

In the 1980's, television sitcoms like the "Cosby Show" strengthened the minds of my generation. According to some members of the Black community, Bill Cosby's sitcom inspired many African American families to think about their lifestyles in broader cultural dimensions. Its spin-off, "A Different World," single-handedly inspired countless adolescent Blacks to venture into college. Many would be among the first in their family to attend (myself included). Both Cosby shows helped to instill a new found consciousness in Black families, not only making it possible for many people to effectively cope, but overcome the negative consequences of oppression or marginalization.

Marginalization in the United States is one reason why minorities and their families undergo cultural stress. Today, they continue to overcome through education, music, and other cultural achievements, shedding light on chronic living conditions that function as potent stressors in their lives. In this way, they reestablish, reaffect, and reaffirm their moral integrity.

In the new millennium, Whites are much more accepting of Blacks compared to the 45 plus years of experience dealing with legislative mandates for racial equality and social justice. They appear to be moving progressively toward liberal racial attitudes and resisting their own discomfort, uneasiness, and fear. Change in attitude is evident. How so? Most White people have come to terms with their own prejudices only to set aside small-minded differences.

The result was the election of our first African American President, Barack Hussein Obama, Jr. Yet, occasional incidents between cultural systems continue to spark conflict and hate: Racial profiling and White police abuse of African Americans continue to reinforce the ills of modernity. Opposing attitudes toward Blacks in America, behind closed doors, serve only to tell people when a society needs are not met, cultural problems will remain unchanged. In any event, static development of culture is one reason why paradoxes occur.

It is uncommon for people to think of ignoble motives as existing paradoxes. Ignoble motives are the remnants of sometimes arbitrary, but generally, quite personal dislikes. James M. Jones once said:

> When the cultural mainstream continues to dislike minorities, it is literately negative feelings left over from a people who learned they share more in common with members of different groups than first imagined.

The psychological significance of these negative feelings is a frustration that contradicts the need for contact. Aversions are ultimately projected onto targeted groups. In this sense, perceived differences in morals, beliefs, and values serve only to justify certain advantages and disadvantages. If, however, we come to understand disliking members from an out-group can be associated with liking members of the in-group, then learning about absurdities and ignoble motives become easy.

26

James M. Jones (1971-1995) saw the relationship between Dale Berra and his father, Yogi, as an existing paradox. His opening statement characterizes the theme found in this book. The increasingly sophisticated reasoning found in this book is much better than the original essay. What I illustrate in each chapter is multiply determined by several factors. In this way, the book gives interested readers important insight into which dimensions of culture influence a continuance of cultural problems.

Each chapter ahead symbolizes not only frustration, but the consequences of stress and coping in dealing with a nation considered hostile. In this way, minorities are forced to endure chronic living conditions, a suffering all too common among African and Hispanic Americans.

Resolving cultural problems in America is the next big challenge. As a nation of opposites, we are influenced by our racial and ethnic ties. Nevertheless, people should be valued and not just for the sake of their similarities as Dale Berra implied. It will take some undoing, though— that is, to make great strides in a nation obsessed with equality, yet fears change. In addition, we need to understand people are more attracted to those who look like them in fear of sharing similarities with individuals perceived as different (odd). In this sense, we begin to understand there are perceived differences that greatly exists not only between, but among cultural groups.

The Ignoble Paradox of Man is an attempt to bring into awareness existing problems between the larger society and smaller cultural groups. Yet, another possibility occurs because we are too late and open dialogue telling truth about the contexts in which minorities live will not help improve people's ability to get along with one another. In this way, there can be no sense of responsibility for community and wellness in the world. Since America is haunted by her discomfort, uneasiness, and fear, the movement forward toward progress enables society to socially resist change. Unfortunately, for the larger society, unwillingness to change is threatened by an even greater fear of responsibility and accountability.

One of the most important themes found in this book is how our absurdities and ignoble motives often form paradoxes. To engage people in lively controversy about absurdities and ignoble motives will help us confront many of the important issues racial and ethnic minorities must endure in their everyday, ordinary lives. People set in comparison are prime reasons why cultural problems cause paradoxes and vice versa.

Paradoxes are not complex phenomena, but concepts of opposites, which arouse inverse reasoning in people. Understanding the problem of paradoxes may help people put cultural problems into proper context. Use this book as a tool to improve on your understanding of absurdities and ignoble motives.

Perhaps your efforts to understand The Ignoble Paradox of Man will be successful. It does provide clues to make learning about life more cordial and enjoyable. What could be more important to us all than learning about our thoughts, feelings, and motives? It may one day help you increase your effectiveness in cooperating with strangers and others. In the end, we should be able to reduce minority pain and suffering from further oppression. As a matter of democracy, it is critical for us all.

As you can see, the book in question has various turns to negotiate. Although this book only briefs my thoughts and interests on sociocultural issues, my hope is after reading it you will take away a new found understanding of how to stimulate positive thinking about intergroup relations in the United States and abroad. I would also like for you to carefully consider resolutions that could help reduce or even eliminate interracial tensions and hostility in Western civilizations.

Here, I hope the content of this book will not in any way misrepresent my intentions. As a researcher and future psychologist, I am committed in my efforts to bring into consideration topics outside of what is ordinarily expected. I vow from this day forth to stay directly involved with issues important to the Black community. For my people, freedom or having the natural ability to choose is an everyday matter of life and death.

Introduction
The Ignoble Paradox of Man

Dark-skinned Blacks in the United States have lower socioeconomic status, more punitive relationships with the criminal justice system, diminished prestige, and less likelihood of holding elective office compared with their lighter counterparts. This phenomenon of "colorism" both occurs within the African American community and is expressed by outsiders, and most Blacks are aware of it. Nevertheless, Blacks' perceptions of discrimination, belief that their fates are linked or attachment to their race almost never vary by skin color. We identify this disparity between treatment and political attitudes as "the skin color paradox," and use it as a window into the politics of race in the United States over the past half century.

Jennifer L. Hochschild (2012)

What discomfort, uneasiness, and fear brought America were two men who contributed their own efforts to a problem, greatly paralyzing the masses. When the newly appointed Attorney General, Erik Holder, gave his now infamous speech, he called for the nation to have open discussions on race matters. "Americans continue to be a nation of cowards," Holder admonished. His address to the nation came not so long after a former pastor to then Democratic nominee and Presidential candidate, Senator Barack Obama, nearly destroyed the hopeful's chance of being elected to the Oval Office. Reverend Jeremiah Wright delivered a disparaging sermon, considered by many to be a hate speech, about Senator Hillary Clinton and her lack of ties to the African American community. Many people felt victimized and unfairly judged by the words of both men.

Other people believed these speeches were noble yet misguided attempts to awaken a great nation to its ugly xenophobic resentment. Yet, somehow, they failed in their delivery to reach everyday, ordinary people. In fact, their speeches were noble since each drove home the point African Americans are frustrated by a duplicity of double standards and differential treatment they endure from a nation considered hostile. Yet, their speeches were misguided, not because it aroused anxiety and fear among communities privy to the mainstay of life, nor from placing Black issues at the forefront of discussion. But, neither speaker included important views on women, lesbians, gays, and other minorities living in America into their speeches.

Further, they failed to link Black issues to community and wellness. In this case, neither Attorney General Holder nor Reverend Wright conveyed a message that would in any way reflect the progressive efforts of modern reform. After all, we witnessed the election of our first African American President who won the popular vote in Iowa, the Whitest State in America. It has become obvious to many people in this country, Americans are beginning to embrace change. However, this monumental upheaval stemming from economic decline, cultural decay, and contempt for the current situation is what I call *"the ignoble paradox of man."*

The 2008 presidential election took place in the fall. The race existed between three candidates. The country was in a terrible recession due to a debauchment that took place in the Bush administration. What seemed like insurmountable odds stacked up against the African

American candidate turned in his favor when the other two running parties miscommunicated their allegiance or intentions. Was this misattempt a failed effort to communicate their intentions of equality?

Two areas in which Republicans appeared to be vulnerable were women and minority rights. By contrast, the minority candidate appeared to be well-versed in politics, community oriented, and had an aptitude for economics. When people learned the Presidential candidate was biracial, the question quickly turned to, "Is he Black enough" for African Americans? "Is he White enough," quickly became the standard by White American comparisons. This election was the first time in US history a minority of any gender or racial mixture was voted into presidency and not by White men, but White women and minorities. The 2008 presidential election was a most important progression not only for US Senator Barack Obama, but women and minorities in their effort to reach full equality.

As more minorities seek to reach higher status, the issue of race is assumed a more important feature. In today's social climate, we are more likely to follow the leadership of those who meet societal standards, especially if they can modify their behavior and experiences to fit the normative expectations of affluent, middle-class White males. A solution to the problem exists in understanding for whom and under what set of circumstances does race make the most difference. If we wanted to find out in what way do minority attitudes, behaviors, appearances, reputations, and experiences influence majority groups in terms of leadership capabilities and responsibilities, such qualities often include features like race and physical attractiveness to reach a final conclusion.

In contrast, White men, not women, discriminated against the minority candidate. Curiously, White men seeing minorities as less qualified also failed to elect Senator Hillary Clinton into office during the 2008 Presidential election. Might her efforts to have a Grateful Dead concert at Woodstock amid an economic recession be the reason why she did not meet their behavioral expectations on valued dimensions? Race was a salient factor in how people voted that year, but not the underlying reason.

Events surrounding the 2008 Presidential election were most important to Americans. Why so? Their needs had not been met. Anti-female bias among middle-class White males was offset by the allegiance of White women and minorities dedicated to establishing their equal rights. Women sought to vote for President Obama. Why? They experienced inequality during past presidencies, which left them vulnerable with regard to their independence. Arguably, attractiveness became a prime factor for women and minorities, especially when many found out Senator Barack Obama, a White-Black biracial male lawyer, was educated at Harvard University.

Most of us cannot begin to understand what happened in 2008. Why so? We cave in under the ways of sophisticated society. Open discussions held by conservatives and liberals show how hopelessly ensnared we are in our misunderstanding of race. At best, the impressive way network syndicate displayed the Presidential campaign, witnessed in full public view, is an assertion offering firsthand authentication to just how morally debilitated our views of race are in America.

Attempts to masquerade racism as Chicago style politics underscored the complexity of racial discourse, and how we Americans disguise our own psychopathologies as legitimate expressions. The amount of political bashing from presidential candidates was so numerous that for weeks, months even, each nominee took turns in trying to reduce the only African American candidate to a permanent underclass. What was predictable about race-baiting conservatives and liberals against the only racial minority candidate was their willingness to portray him as incompetent and incapable of making an informed decision. The subtle, yet sophisticated ways we depict race in America greatly contributes to the intellectual limitations of Western culture.

To engage in a serious discourse on The Ignoble Paradox of Man we must concern ourselves not with social problems, which affect people from all walks of life, but the intellectual limitations of Western politics. America was founded on the basic principles of Democratic theory, which states all people being equal under God shall enjoy their inalienable rights to life, liberty, and the pursuit of happiness. However, Republicanism appears to be the catalyst that causes Western culture's intellectual limitations. That is to say, their support for general principles of equality may be superficial.

For instance, while it appears the Republican Party strongly support liberal practices like racial integration, same-sex marriage, and minority hiring, this may be lip service. It may simply be their formal concerns, opinions, and assumptions about equality are discussed in the abstract. It is easy to talk cordially about equality, but supporting it has costly implications. So long as members of the Republican Party are set in conflict or competition with minorities, they will continue to plague the best of our society.

The intellectual limitations of Republicanism or Post Party Conservatism includes people's debilitating views of change and how discomfort, uneasiness, and fear trigger our greatest problem of inequality—unfairness. Conservatives, for instance, boast about their effort to preserve the best in society while opposing radical change. However, their egalitarian concept of equality for all is masked by the conservative notion that if minorities are to be accepted in society, they must be well behaved. Some people believe the egalitarian values boasted by conservative Republicans are at odds with the historical facts. In this way, they may purposely undergo the preservation of long-established customs and institutions to resist change.

Too often *conservatives* or those favoring Western tradition have taken clear advantage of their situation. In seeking to justify their own biases, they often exploit, oppress, or humiliate people from various societies. Might those averse to change create a strong need to uphold traditional values? Women too were historically oppressed by those said to firmly support equality, which meant a world of restrictions, barriers, and unfair treatment.

Can conservatives adapt to the social requirements of current times? Cultural adaptation depends on recognizing and respecting legitimate differences among various racial and ethnic groups. Conservatives often say they would never break from traditional values. They also say conservatives felt a significant departure from modern concepts or propositions. However, it is important to remember that as far back as 1937-1963 conservatives played a key role in the Conservative Coalition that controlled Congress. In the past, during the era of racial segregation and social injustice, many Southern Democrats were members of the Conservative Party. Since the 1950's, however, Republicans in the United States are largely associated with conservatism.

Drs. John Dovidio and S.L. Gaertner (1986), authors of a book entitled Prejudice, Discrimination, and Racism, believe Whites (conservatives) appear to have a genuine ambivalence about Blacks. This notion draws from the understanding that conservatives are averse to change. As a result, they may experience conflict between their genuinely egalitarian values and own negative feeling toward Black Americans. Their conflict causes them to experience shame. Coupled with the understanding they may not want Black people to know, the shame experienced causes them to develop avoidance behavior.

Further, David O. Sears (1987) said in his book Symbolic Racism, attempts to condition Blacks so they will not push hard and fast for equality, make unfair demands, and get undeserved special attention like gainful employment, better housing opportunities, or request the right to better education, clearly shows the nature of Whites. He called the continued attitude of anti-Black feelings and traditional values, like those held by followers of the Protestant ethic, symbolic racism.

Curiously, some conservatives sympathize with Black people. They recognize problems Black Americans once confronted and continue to confront, but feel they contribute to their own plight. The predicament of Blacks in America, they believe, is caused by a lack of ambition and failure to take advantage of opportunities. In this way, we gain a clear understanding of how intergroup relations destabilize.

Also, the Democratic Party does not go without scrutiny for their mishandling of intergroup relations. In a social media post, Michelle Alexander pointed out that for too long the Democratic Party dealt with Blacks as if they were political refugees with nowhere else to live. Democrats treat Black people as if they were to leave the Democratic Party then certain political wolves, calling themselves Republicans, would devour them. Well, Black people are tired of taking part in an election that calls on them to vote for the lesser of two evils, Michelle reasoned.

Michelle also pointed out that Black activists from the Black Lives Matter movement (#BLM) are showing Black people they do not have to play out the political-hand politics deals them. They have a wide range of options available for them. These activists remind people that Blacks do not have to vote Republican or Democratic. They can opt to create a political movement, form a new political party, or have a revolution.

For instance, decades of oppression and state-sponsored violence against young Black Baltimoreans led to a revolt against police authority. Although the government allowed racial tensions to build for decades, the result was cultural awareness brought to a critical problem that destabilized intergroup relations. Now I realize the revolt was poorly planned; and, it was premature. But, it sparked a political upsurge of nonviolent disobedience, political mobilization of resources, and moral suasion to mobilize public opinion.

Now, I do not advocate violence as a means to resolve conflict. That's not my argument. But, thanks to racial tensions and hostility mounting between Whites and Blacks in America, an increasing amount of poor Black people are opting for change.

Change can be turbulent and could alter the current state of affairs. In this regard, acculturating Blacks fear change. Instead, they work to preserve the status quo. Acculturating Blacks are comfortable voting for politicians who will bring the least amount of change to their lifestyles. Since many have established themselves in the cultural mainstream, they do not want to be involved in a political movement that could change the way they live in today's society. What's ignoble about acculturating Blacks and American politicians therein is their inability to confront the tragic facts of life. Both tear at the very fabric of American democracy.

Now, in order to free ourselves of any restrictions that develop from Western politics' intellectual limitations, we must understand all internal struggles. To contend resolutely with our internal struggles is more difficult than understanding the establishment of new social classes, new social conditions, and new struggles that often replace old ones. In this way, the 2008 presidential election was not a cure-all for problems of inequality.

The 2008 Presidential election did not ease our subjective concerns about racial inequality. Nor did it relieve any fears the public had about a falling economy. Although Senator Barack Obama was the best qualified candidate to elect for presidency, people understood that racial inequality would not waste away simply with his election. As well, conservative Republicans continued to badger him on petty issues rather than help the newly elected President rebuild America's economy. His place of origin and racial identity are two such provincials often in request of authentication.

What the election did accomplish, though, would teach Americans a valuable lesson. People learned how to set aside their small-minded differences for the sake of common good even when they, in some way, fear being disadvantaged. Here, people often ask the question, "What's ignoble about the paradox of man?" I say unto you the hope of civilization is conditioned on whether there exists a greater inequality that plagues humanity.

On Tuesday, January 20, 2009, before a massive crowd celebrating in a moment of historical significance, Senator Barack Hussein Obama, Jr. was admitted into the Presidential Oval Office. As America's 44th President, his induction held at the United States Capitol in Washington, DC, was the only mistake in a near perfect inaugural ceremony. However, when the solemn oath was administered to then President-elect Obama in his public inauguration ceremony, a single word, "faithfully," was misplaced. Failure to give proper attention or thought to administering the oath aroused apprehension among people.

Many people, particularly African Americans, asked why the solemn oath was botched for the first Black President. In the past, Whites never considered African Americans for presidency based on the cultural stereotype all Black people are unintelligent. Might the manner in which Chief Justice John Roberts Jr. administered the oath be a continuation of this mental attitude? Failure to acknowledge the natural abilities of African Americans led to widespread social injustice. Such unfairness or inequality continues to threaten the humanity of Blacks.

The vast majority of Whites support President Obama, our Commander-in-Chief. However, occasional incidents still spark conflict and hatred among various racial and ethnic groups. For instance, US Army Major Nidal Malik Hasan killed 13 US soldiers at Fort Hood, Texas, wounding 30 in the process.

President Obama was accused of being un-American for this particular incident. Conservatives believed since the President has a Muslim surname, he would cater to radial Muslims and terrorist groups. As a result, they used Christianity to level accusations directed at him. Why? Many felt "the Nobel Peace Prize winning President" let a terrorist attack take place on United States soil. Yet, in a similar vein, no one roused the former President—with the exception of African Americans and a few conscious Muslims—for letting al Qaeda murder more than five thousand US citizens on his oval watch.

Former President George Bush, Jr., who by the way, retreated well into hiding during the 9/11 terrorist attacks in New York, Pennsylvania, and Washington, DC was, himself, hailed a hero by conservatives and Republicans. In a conversation with David Sanger, author of the book <u>Confront and Conceal: Obama's Secret Wars and Surprising use of American Power</u>, David Rothkope asked, *"How much credit do you think George Bush and his team deserve for what is now characterized as the Obama doctrine?"* Sanger replied by saying President Obama deserves much of the credit for rethinking, realistically, what our overall strategy was in Middle Eastern Asia.

Apparently, circumstances surrounding the 9/11 events led to the loss of 1 million Iraqi soldiers and citizens along with a national deficit of about 16 trillion, US made, hard earned American tax dollars. Former President George Bush Jr. also drove America into the worst economic recession since the Great Depression.

As a continuation, America hailed federal police Sergeant (Sgt.) Kimberly Munley heroine after eyewitness accounts failed to conclude she stopped the Fort Hood, Texas shooter. Curiously, no government agency acknowledged the African American male and partner to Sgt. Munley for his heroic deeds.

Network media failed to disclose it was federal officer Senior Sgt. Mark Todd who actually took down the shooter. The media's intent to make deliberately false statements about the main hero of Fort Hood, Texas is a classic example of how Whites continue to show their contempt and apathy for Blacks living in America. Even after the matter was cleared up on CBS "the Early Show" and later on "Oprah," Whites continued to win praise or attention for Sgt. Munley by preempting Oprah's attempt to obtain credit for Senior Sgt. Mark Todd. White people's mental attitudes toward Black Americans continue to contribute a legacy of hate to their problems.

Conservatives continue to display White xenophobic resentment. Such xenophobia is thought to be caused by Black crime. Now they believe the threat and danger to their way of living will come from terrorist attacks caused by Muslim Americans. Or, will they continue to center their conversation on the urban influx of poor Hispanic immigrants, who by the way are looking more and more like US citizens, as Whites consciously avoid thinking of unwelcomed events taking place on American soil. Either way, the current attitude seems to warrant more discomfort, uneasiness, and fear of change.

Dissonance over the presence and predicaments of Blacks in America led to the notion of color-blindness. The election of our first African American President, along with greater acceptance of interracial and same-sex marriages, is a testimony to this popular notion. Some people engage in lively controversy about whether White America will continue to move forward along the course of modern reform and better racial attitudes. Others believe the success of politically motivated groups like "The Tea Party" shows America cannot reform.

FOX News gave us a typical example when it televised Glenn Beck's assertion that President Barack Obama was a racist with deep seeded hatred toward White people. Similarly, the media went into frenzy over selected excerpts from a speech given to graduate students by Supreme Court Justice Sonia Sotomayor. During a Senate Judiciary Committee hearing, Congress openly challenged her method of delivery. Afterward, they blatantly ask the then Supreme Court Justice nominee if she was racist against White people. Supreme Court Justice Sotomayor responded, wittingly, by saying she was better suited to hear the concerns of minorities than people having little if any interactions with them.

The whole theoretical notion of a color-blinded society is dangerous and difficult to grasp. It implies White people are unable to adequately deal with minorities in broader cultural dimensions. That any attempt to reach full equality is based on how well Whites learn to ignore skin color. Apparently, they feel skin color or one's primary physical characteristic is an impaired trait or condition, causing people emotional distress. Well, if conservatives are to void themselves of prejudice, discrimination, and racial preference, they will simply have to set aside their natural discomfort, uneasiness, and inherent fear of change. Otherwise minorities, particularly Black Americans, will continue to have difficulty reaching full equality.

Question: How do we continue to progress beyond the intellectual limitations of Western culture? America and its citizens must continue, with certainty, to grasp a better understanding that the ability to bring about change lies within ourselves. People must come to realize discomfort, uneasiness, and fear transmits through the presence and limitations of prejudice and discrimination. Yet, racial preference is not so much a problem as opposed to being extremely homogenized in one's way of thinking. In short, the hypothetical concept of a color-blinded or post-racial society proposes danger for us all. Resolution should not reside around one's refusal to acknowledge an unacceptable realism or unpleasant emotion, but rest on compassion, affection, or greater feelings toward people in order to affect change.

Today's youth have chosen to take action toward achieving change. Despite our disregard for their public wellness, chronic living conditions such as poverty and unemployment places many youth at risk for crime and other antisocial involvement. Today, the younger generation shows remarkable adaptiveness, resilience, and responsibility in their quest for equality. This quest involves developing a peaceful identity and awareness of one's own individuality. In the long run, we as adults will simply have to face the actual factuals of equality and that is a cultural meshing of customs and social demands, stemming from competition, encourage our youth to change.

In what way has the younger generation changed? That's another good question! Despite the unfortunate history of many adolescents today, they are more sensitive to the vulnerabilities of negative stereotypes communicated against members of other cultural groups. Adolescents today also refuse to be hampered by their immigrant origins in that many are affluent or literate in English. They also value interaction with various cultural groups, and may have lifestyles that differ from mainstream society.

Included in these changes is the role of cultural expectations. For the most part, immigrant groups are relegated to minority status. Mainstream society inconvenienced these groups by protecting them under the false cloth of paternalism. Paternalism essentially denies their freedoms and responsibilities. Well, the conservative attitude of paternalism appears not to be the case for today's youth. Young Americans in the coming generation already upset mainstream culture when they challenged the status quo by electing their choice for Presidential Office. After all, communities' privy to the mainstay of life, whose agenda includes exclusion of those having skin color or customs different from their own, can no longer be fortified against minorities.

In contrast, negative portrayal of young Americans who live in inner cities reveal many as cognitively unaware. They are said not to be affluent or literate, have little or no understanding of family as a support system, do not adhere to the American work ethic, and have no use for politics. Their plight is said to be further eroded by the unfortunate history of discrimination. Many people believe the government took this opportunity to enhance their suffering. This form of tragedy requires we treat them not as burdens, but develop better opportunities to work in education and healthcare while continuing to build stronger community support. In this way, some experts believe their needs will have a greater chance of being met.

Some young adults today define minority roles as important to the intellectual achievement of Western culture. Such acclaims include their contributions in the areas of music, economic growth, and Civil Rights. For instance, Black activists and White progressives like Former President John F. Kennedy have bettered society by establishing merit based career opportunities for themselves, women, Asians, and other minorities. Pioneers like singer and activist Harry Belafonte, lynching activist Ida B. Wells-Barnett, the late great Markus Garvey, Black Nationalist Malcolm X, Dr. Martin Luther King, Jr., DD, Rosa Parks, American politician, educator, and author Shirley Anita St. Hill Chisholm, and a laundry list of others would be among the many who made contributions in ways that would forever change the tapestry of American culture.

Allow me to digress. Shirley Anita St. Hill Chisholm greatly contributed to changing how White Americans perceive Blacks. She became the first African American Congresswoman. She was also a crusader in the fight for racial equality. She later campaigned for the Democratic presidential nomination. But due to her outspoken nature, Congresswoman Shirley Chisholm would fail to influence potential supporters in the election polls.

As a Civil Rights activist and radical, Ida B. Wells-Barnett single-handedly stopped Black people from being lynched in America. She was murdered at age 63, poisoned with arsenic by her neighborhood grocery store butcher. A little known fact about Ida is her brainchild, which later became the NAACP.

Despite a wealth of achievements, Black people's social status has yet to improve. Their contributions have done little, if any, to change the thinking strategies of mainstream culture. As a result, Black people are among the poorest in the United States. Thirty-point-two percent of the Black population below the age of eighteen years lived in poverty before the new millennium. Numbers have increased considerably since then. Although poverty translates to school failure, less than adequate healthcare, and contributes to problems in developing a positive identity, many young adults believe minorities continue to bring about important change. Today's youth continues to show awareness for the values and norms needed to achieve change in America. And, that level of consciousness is good for everyone.

There is something ignoble about the paradox of man. We have a narrow-minded concept of humanity. Imbued with an aggressively misguided value system, people from all walks of life are comfortably deluded by an exaggerated estimate of their abilities to interact. However, if we are to invest in a better understanding of culture, people must first ascertain what makes us civil-minded. Why? Not one person can afford to limit his or her preference or choice for which race he or she will consider.

We are becoming citizens of the world, interconnected through communication and commerce. What we must do is change the public opinion, knock down old barriers, and buildup new structures. In this way, we reduce the continuing threat of racial ignorance that causes undue suffrage among Blacks and other minorities. By seeking out equality, we reinvest in what's good about the changing tapestry American culture.

The election of our first Black President serves as proof people are able to change. The man who delivered us Osama Bin Laden, reduced terrorist activity in the Middle East, and paved the way for democracy in Libya, is a great testament to those realizations. His election is indeed a great monument in our attempts to push beyond Western culture's intellectual limitations. It also proves we are capable of changing and satisfying our own needs.

Chapter 1
The Concept of Racial Inequality in Conservative White America

Success breeds conservatism, and that means a love affair with the status quo and an aversion to change.

Frank Popoff (1935-)

What I find to be most troubling about conservatives in the United States is their natural discomfort, uneasiness, and fear of change. Just when they appear to be making gradual improvement in progress and reform, many fall below the expectations of decency often displayed among moderates and liberals. For African Americans, the murder of Trayvon Martin on February 26, 2012, raised doubt about conservatives and their less than accepting attitude toward Black children. Inattention from Florida authorities as well as White political and clergy leaders confirmed their mental attitude. Not even during the Civil Rights movement has equality for Blacks, Hispanics, and other minorities been a part of their agenda.

For conservatives, the paradox of racial inequality involves a duplicitous representation. Often in bad faith, except in public spaces where they make socially correct comments about minorities, many continue to discriminate, behind closed doors even. Thus, the idea of conservatism developing from a people who share in cultural knowledge and values advocating what's best for society becomes an intriguing and interesting thought.

We all understand it is nearly impossible to discuss inequality without bringing up the concept of race. Yet, most White researchers who examine racial inequality and social injustice conduct their investigations with little or no reference to how it influences conservative White Americans. In my thesis, I propose racial inequality is a taboo topic among conservative Whites. In this way, the larger dominant society continues to experience discomfort, uneasiness, and fear of change. Here, an open dialogue telling truth about its unspoken nature becomes necessary for minorities to reach full equality.

A major impact in the Trayvon Martin case was Black America's call for racial equality and social justice. However, the lack of moral response from White Americans aroused tension among Blacks. Religious leaders like reverends Al Shapten and Jessie Jackson expressed a need for spiritual union between White and Black churches. They felt if ever there was a time for churches to unite in solidarity, tragic events like Trayvon Martin's murder could build a union of interest, purpose, or sympathy for the greater good of humanity.

Reverends Sharpten and Jackson contend a religious union among members of various congregations has the potential to bring Whites in closer contact with other racial and ethnic groups. As well, coming together could facilitate more social learning. In contrast, joining together with various White politicians and Church congregations during such a tragic time may not lead to shared feelings on valued dimensions. Yet, when people unite for the greater good of humanity, the result is often spatial relations whereby humane interaction occurs.

To make the plight of Blacks known to Whites in America is requisite for healthy intergroup relations. In

Trayvon's case, the lack of moral response to such a travesty sent demoralizing and dehumanizing messages across cultures. People from various societies, who share common histories of oppression and degradation, would unite in genuine empathy and principal criticisms.

There is nothing more encouraging than to see people unite through the broad complex development of intergroup relations. However, people cannot begin to come together if they are distracted by the dismissive attitude of conservatism found among Republicans in White leadership. However, their leadership cannot afford to overlook the heterogeneity of popular culture in their fifty year quest for national solidity.

Curiously, conservative leaders, in failing to properly address the matter of Trayvon Martin—that is, the lack of prayers dedicated to Trayvon and his family during televised political, clergy, and evangelist programming— showed a personal disregard for Black people. Sadly, Blacks are largely disregarded even though they're often congregation members in the White church. There was not even a mention from Pat Robinson and The 700 Club, a religious television program that promotes core White values and conservative ideals of Christian fundamentalism, in response to the Trayvon Martin travesty.

As with the case of so many differences in human behavior, religious motivation remains an important experience for people. That is, religion has important supremacy underpinnings. Specifically, the word White has always been strongly associated with public Christian worship as in morally or spiritually pure. Why does religion strongly imply a person whose interests follow life under monastic vows is more connected with God, for instance? Religious motivation compels us to pursue life free from impurities with reverence and devotion. Those who worship are seen as supreme followers of institutionalized religion with pristine moral values and ethics, said to exist in a blissful state or whiteness.

On the other end of the spectrum are those who fail to worship. They are viewed as hesitant people or blackened heathens. The two color schemes closely relate to an existing division between Caucasians and Africans. The color "white" was chosen as a racial identity to be used by Caucasians after abandoning all European terms like Englishmen, Puritan, and Christian free. Caucasians renamed themselves "White man." Why? They were supposed to exist in higher religious supremacy as evident by their phenotype. Many considered their phenotype an affect of God. Hence, the color "black" was used to characterize Africans and American Negroes whose physical appearances were thought to be an obvious manifestation of an unholy race. Their phenotype was associated with a "blackened" heathenish state or supreme evil spirit. So, Christian religion is thought to reaffirm White ideals of racial supremacy.

Now, my intention is neither to demonize Whites nor the church. However, the easiest way to induce a state of inferiority in people is to threaten them with condemnation. It's crucial to understand that the fundamental basis of religious devotion is predicated on myths about interaction, especially with people who are thought to differ on valued dimensions. Along with instilling the fear of God in church members and condemning hell bound heathens (trifles found in institutionalized religions), the church serves only to convince minorities they are inherently underdeveloped and less civilized than White people.

Physical slavery, lynching, and the system of segregation that terrorized quite a few people were put into place and carried out precisely to devalue Black people. Such disparagement challenged their human dignity. Many, now broken spirited by a continuous devaluation and degradation of their dignity, adopt the social norms and behavioral expectations of their oppressor. Why? We often internalize our fears because of the real or imagined pressure to conform. New recruiting strategies in White supremacy work better than many research experts—people adept on the intimacies of racism and racial discrimination—understand.

For instance, problems associated with racial supremacy do not develop by hate or racism alone. Essentially, the movement is motivated by wealth, power, and income. Racism is simply one of many tools used to scare people into a theater of fantasies. Similarly, the church alone cannot provide the motivation needed to effect change in one's way of thinking. What's needed is a pattern of fear. Actually, Christian church uses hate and fear as motivations to create conformity, distance groups from one another, and develop the bourgeois mentality often displayed among conservatives living in middle-class America today.

Needless to say, many people continue to hold Black dignity in low-regard. The lack of regard occurs because Black accomplishments and other manifestations of their intellectual achievement are condemned by the White church. As a result, some Whites continue to view segregation as a wholesome American value system. In contrast, the birth of rock'n roll, hip hop culture, and popular music caused many people to look deep within and to seek out universal interaction in their quest for sameness or solidarity. Such interaction is true even if exaggerated tails of violence and criminal behavior about Black people persist.

I see this quest as a natural progression of evolution. That whenever people meet for the purpose of interaction, a positive outcome will occur. Yet, so long as cultural perception is based on mythic tails of the problematic minority, conservatives will continue to show aversion toward change. In fact, what we have here is a dilemma of mythology and morality. Such a dilemma impedes our natural ability to evolve as social creatures.

Why did Whites support George Zimmerman in the wrongful death of Trayvon Martin? That's a good question! Many people said high crime and violence in the Black community gave White supporters reason to believe his public cries were possible ideas of innocence. In this way, the overwhelming financial assistance Zimmerman received was merely an act of good faith. However, his supporters were more likely showing protest for government legislation that passed in favor of increased healthcare, minority rights, et cetera.

Let me explain. Initiatives Present Obama proposed were, as they claim, too radical for conservatives. On the surface, many felt new revisions to medical insurance policies under "Obamacare" would, in some way, affect the financial stability and social security of hard working American citizens. However, upon closer inspection, many believed new mandates in healthcare constituted reparations for Black people; and they, in no way, wanted to make amends for the wrongdoings of past Whites. In this way, the recession was a legitimate reason to keep Black people disadvantaged.

As for Zimmerman, the support he received was an extension of contempt Whites have for the competency, capability, and possibility of Black people. To put it bluntly, they despise minorities, especially Blacks. But if you ask conservatives whether they support minority rights to important access, they cope with their discontent by denying it. For instance, most lie when asked whether they support social programs that will help minorities succeed in the larger society. This tendency is at best fascinating, especially in its extremity. In short, there is dissension among Republicans, a bitterly opposed school of thought, clearly indisposed to helping minorities.

Dissenters argue, emphatically, minorities who do not pay into tax relieve funds will plague our already overburdened and unresponsive bureaucratic systems. They believe problems of financial, housing, and health assistance already contributes to America's outstanding loan obligations. And such problems place hard working citizens at risk. Subjective concerns for change bring wealth to the center of White discussion. Minorities, on the other hand, must learn to cope with more problems of poverty and discrimination. Concerns may be especially stressful for dissenters who seek out separation while Republicans in the coming generation learn to cope with integration.

Subjective concerns are also related to threatening and uncontrollable life events. For instance, the recession means some middle-class citizens will have to experience poverty. Many who experience poverty will suffer discrimination, and from members of their own community. Feelings of alienation evoke glandular aversions to materialistic changes in value. In this way, dissenters are unsupportive of liberal attitudes toward modern changes in progress and reform.

However, beyond any impersonal statistics, there are people whose lives are greatly affected. Healthcare, diet and nutrition, and education lay at the brut of this issue—not whether they can continue to make payment on a new Jaguar or dedicate Friday evening as pizza night to enjoy quality time with their children—economic decisions privy to the rich and affluent middle-class. Curiously, young

Republicans are willing to mainstream minorities into the larger society if they uphold Western tradition or core White values. In this way conservatives, low progressing for the sake of caution, can also benefit from change.

Certainly, we know not every American is equal. We also know Whites as well as politically connected people pass advantages to their children while minorities and poor people pass disadvantages to their children. Further, we know life chances for a Hispanic girl born to migrant workers differ immensely from a girl born to American parents who are wealthy and well-educated. Since we know this to be true, America developed social programs to make opportunities more available. Affirmative Action, college scholarships, and community colleges are attempts to help level the playing field. However, these opportunities become problematic for minorities living in cultures obsessed with equality yet fear change.

The United States has a healthy preoccupation with racial equality. But, in other ways, it is haunted by its fear of change. White Americans, particularly conservatives, embrace equality but fear change. How could that statement possibly be true? The establishment of racial equality puts forward realistic responses to modern reform. Black Democrats emphasize this point, in particular, by trying to discredit conservative White leadership. They say that the real problem with modern reform is Republicans and their political agenda.

For instance, Democrats said the Republican strategy was, as Senate Majority Leader Mitch McConnell (R-KY) puts it, to commit all efforts into making Barrack Obama a one-term president. Then there was Congressman Bobby Schilling (R-Ill.), a Tea Party member, who neither in the past nor present had a clue about Republicans' diabolical game plan to sabotage every initiative President Obama attempted, including improving the economy. Congressman Schilling failed to understand Republicans tried to undermine the political position of Black liberals. They wanted to counteract liberals by replacing them with minority members of the Republican Party. They even wanted to use conservative Black Democrats—who subvert government policies by pushing strategies to enhance market structure and function—while stressing success-oriented values in low income Black communities.

If minorities, particularly African Americans, fail in their efforts to reduce the threat of racial inequality, then they will become as vulnerable as those in the past. In this case, their efforts will become disruptive and a certain fate awaits them. In this way, if Blacks, in their struggle to reach full equality, continue to be distracted by conservative strategies, instead of gaining equal status among America's so-called cultural elite, they will become further disadvantaged.

In this way, conservatives like Newt Gingrich and Mitt Romney, who reaffirm stand-your-ground gun laws as well as lobby against woman and minority rights, will continue to endorse discriminatory policies that increase

Black people's suffering or social misery. Certainly, today's Black youth do understand that prejudice and discrimination are woeful reasons for their situation. However, they also realize neither one is the main problem source in their lives. Thus, most minorities as well as members of dominant White society perceived conservative attacks on President Obama to be rather trite.

Since Black people are thought to have morally objectionable behavior that cause Whites to espouse equality in the abstract, then just because they continue to move forward toward liberalism and better racial attitudes, let the evil they do live on after them, even while their support for general principles of gay rights are somewhat misguided.

So, what about Mr. Zimmerman? Why was he found not guilty? Evidence presented in the case was overwhelmingly in his favor. Yes, that much is true. But, you must first ask yourself how a mother from Jacksonville, Florida can be sentenced to twenty years in prison after stopping a physical attack committed by her husband.

Marissa Alexander was married to Rico Gray, a man who had a history of committing domestic violence. Mrs. Alexander was sentenced to two decades in a Florida State prison for firing what she said was a "warning shot" into the wall to deter her husband from committing spousal abuse. She was denied Florida's stand-your-ground gun law.

Yet, George Zimmerman, the man who shot and killed seventeen-year-old Trayvon Martin, was found not guilty! Well, with a jury of his peers, was there ever any doubt? Five White women and one Hispanic woman found the White and Hispanic biracial man not guilty. However, from day one of the prosecution, a few African Americans believed Florida State prosecutors had no intentions of winning the murder case. In fact, what they believed was prosecutors were going to create a type of side show circus to satisfy Black people's need for racial equality and social justice. Further, they reasoned it would be members of mainstream culture, duped by media's glitzy and glamorous news coverage, who believed the new millennium would bring forth some remnants of change.

How does one come to terms with tragedies like the Trayvon Martin case? What role does the middle-class play in accepting and affirming a people despised by society? Can Blacks have functional relationships while living in male dominant White society even though they are continuously put down, held in low regard, and oppressed to the very end-point of learned hopelessness? A serious response to these perplexing questions require a close inspection into the closed ranks of middle-class White America, a task that demands stimulating information and meaning to be uncovered in an unprecedented manner.

Uncovering the unspoken truth to which many Black intellectuals subscribe in the quest for knowledge, ironically, from perpetrators of their oppression, proposes a fundamental challenge that compels us to recognize our

66

undifferentiated consciousness. The notion of self-concept and esteem requires that Black people need not be preoccupied with conservatism. Yet, the concept of White privy indicates a serious problem. Although private discourse, inside information, and cultural secrecy characterize conservatism or middle-class White American male supremacy, Blacks should not become pessimistic as they once were in the sixties.

Instead, the coming generation should look for more effective and sometime appealing solutions. They may find better strategies to combat White supremacy rather than allowing it to destroy their self-concept and esteem. Similarly, the basis of conservatism is preserving White dignity. In this way, they channel their discomfort, uneasiness, and fear in political and religious directions. This consciousness emerged so conservatives could protect their self-esteem, and at the expense or consideration of Black people.

The historic role of middle-class White America was born out of a progressive effort to redistribute measures that could enhance the quality of living. Such redistribution of measures increased opportunities for disadvantaged Whites. *de facto* Affirmative Action was one such measure of the past that progressed out of preferential policies: Promoting Whites working in domestic capacity to trustee, foreman, and overseer over indentured Blacks and slaves, under a system of racial oppression, denied important opportunities to those whose skills, crafts, and trades placed many in high demand. New opportunities broaden access to America's prosperity for disadvantaged Whites.

Later, Whites acquiring the skills, crafts, and trades, simply placed greater demand on America's prosperity thereby attempting to redistribute wealth, power, and income in their favor. Compromises and concessions were made but only after progressives and liberals pushed for substantive redistributive measures, making opportunities available for them and other disadvantaged Whites.

In early America, progressives were nobleman in their profession thus not entitled to a share of wealth, power, or income. Noblemen consisted of educators, lawyers, doctors, and those belonging to this group. New standards and the quality of living were reached only after lengthy protest in open courts and campaigning on public streets helped them to obtain whatever entitlements and opportunities, especially benefits, felt rightfully due. Forever considered the meddling sort, many prospered from compromises and concessions that included policies like granting contracts, rights to operate subsidiary businesses, and increased income for people whose livelihood were important for the operation of American society. Unfortunately, the effort to reach middle-class status has since been based on preferential policies.

Preferential policies have since contributed to the belief and opinion Blacks, Jews, and immigrant Whites were born as a result of inferior breeding. One way to eliminate this perceived problem was to advance a series of organized actions developed from social Darwinism. Called the eugenics movement, it was a social exclusion and persecution method used to help improve human hereditary traits through controlled breeding.

Eugenic techniques included enforced racial hygiene, human experimentation, along with the extermination of less well-adapted individuals and those considered objectionable. It advanced an idea of structure and behavior, giving purpose to those who opposed racial integration. Under this particular ideology, policies would regulate who should be allowed to conceive and bear children. To resolve this problem, two solutions resulted, segregation and sterilization.

During World War II, intelligence testing quickly became a way to confirm the basis of inferiority in Jews from all societies along with East Germans. By that time, an estimated 44% of Austrian psychiatric physicians joined Hitler's Nazi SS and the eugenics movement. After World War II, eugenics quickly became associated with German Nazism and American racism. In the United States, emancipating Black Americans from segregation (1967) encouraged many conservative supporters to make one last ditch effort in hopes of controlling minorities.

The implication for freeing people from racial impurities—like not being mixed or adulterated with any other racial or genetic material—was seen as an attempt to maintain health and prevent disease. Developments in genetics and human reproduction technology raised many new questions about eugenics as a moral issue of ethics. The belief that human control would be made available only on prescription was enough to justify the fundamental nature of intelligent and unintelligent people. For America, the eugenics movement officially ended in 1975.

Conservatism, which characterizes supremacy in theory, research, and practice, has long been a strong influence of affluent, middle-class, White American males. Therefore, any changes in America regarding equality and justice must come from a people who recognize the significance of racial derision among mainstream Americans in addition to preferential policies. For instance, the merit based system of Affirmative Action was established in 1961 to ensure women and other minorities are treated equally without regard to race, sex, class, religion, or national origin.

Equal opportunity employment now consists of advertising job interviews in public media forums, mandated minimal skill requirements, and prohibitions against quotas. Changes in the job market increased opportunities for qualified women and other minorities. Ironically, today's middle-class Whites benefit from Affirmative Action more than Blacks and other minorities. More importantly, White women are the greatest benefactors. One such measure can be viewed in terms of economic employment.

White women share in many of the same privileges as affluent White men. They also tend to have the same cultural interests as their American male counterparts. White women, who now rank among top professionals, earn a minimum income of about $65k, annually. In the new millennium, White women are the most gainfully employed people in Western society. Educators, doctors, and business professionals are only a few professions in which Affirmative Action helps White women acquire gainful employment. Although they now rank among America's cultural elite, they continue to be viewed as minorities in male dominated White society.

Curiously, women around the world are not known to be motivated by supremacy in frequencies greater than men. The male-female ratio is thought to range from about 9:1 among Americans and higher in most other multicultural countries. In contrast, some researchers now believe women rate among males adopting supremacist beliefs at a ratio of about 3:1. Three explanations for gender differences in supremacy are (1) White women are more likely to demonstrate passive-aggression and, therefore, are less likely to be labeled supremacist; (2), there may exist biological differences between males and females that disposes women to certain behaviors less comparable to males; and (3), life-cycle forces: Different rearing environments, gender-role expectancies, and/or less opportunities, may contribute to nonsupremacist appearances for women than men. Some researchers also theorize social status as a historical factor in women appearing less like supremacist. Or, it may exist as a cover, masking important differences in response to men.

Here, I offer an explanation for life-cycle forces of supremacy found to exist among White women, interpreted as followed:

71

- Supremacy in women is attributable to avoidance and passive-aggressive patterns of behavior; it is also focused on child-rearing, birth control, and education, instead of taking action and learning strategy.
- Gender and sexual identity are part of liberation; so, women are more likely to engage in overt behavior in the new millennium than previous years; such behavioral patterns are major factors of supremacy in women; and, what looks like emotional distress in women may be patterns of racial aggression, moderate or atypical.
- Independence from achieving higher socioeconomic status among women often serves as a protective buffer against stress caused by men. Independent women are less likely to feel vulnerable to males, and greater competition may contribute to increased supremacy in them.
- Wealth is a pathway to independence and supremacy; professional and gender dominant women are thought to be among those who are high-risk for developing supremacist beliefs; socioeconomic status also merits careful consideration.

Supremacy, as an issue and strategy for White women, needs to be addressed. To achieve healthy, nonsupremacist beliefs among them, both social and economic contexts need to be taken into careful consideration. Poor social skills, racial preferences, and culture shock, caused by a suddenly upsetting or surprising experience, can accompany people. Each has important implications.

Culture shock is associated mainly with affluent, middle-class White males from Western cultures. As well, achieving independence through social competition appears to change role expectations. Change in expectations also increases the danger of supremacy manifesting in women. Understanding supremacy in women increases the complexity or difficulty of establishing positive intergroup relations and merit special attention. Perhaps, official efforts to understand supremacy in women will increase the likelihood of bettering intergroup relations with conservative Whites.

Discomfort, uneasiness, and fear are dimensions of racism. Therein, weakness lies in the telling of this unspoken truth. A few applied researchers believe conflicts White people experience between their egalitarian values and own negative feelings toward Blacks is often the reason why they separate themselves from smaller, less dominant cultural groups. Understanding this psychological concept is critical for minorities.

Why so do you ask? It seems conservative Whites are hiding behind the scenes of American racism, fighting against racial equality and social justice. Indeed, conservatives contribute to the misery and wretchedness of suffering found to exist among minorities and their families. Their social misery is often marked out by poverty and inferior living conditions. Yet, racial equality cannot be found on the social, political, or economic agenda of conservatives.

The anger engendered in this truth impedes any meaningful alliance with progressive Whites like Senator Barbara Mikulski, member of the Democratic Party. She was a true progressive and champion of equality. Such an obstruction is responsible for the undeniable legacy of racism found to exist in Western cultures. In contrast, the quest for racial equality involves fairness and justice, concepts inseparable from, yet not identical to, social awareness and cultural literacy.

Without multiracial alliances, a progressive discussion about the future of racial equality will sound like White supremacist ideals we oppose or reject. As for travesties like the Trayvon Martin case, time, history, and culture dictate supporters continue to unite through broad moral vision and greater political organization. In this way, Blacks can make greater efforts to stop the angst that enhance their suffering.

In the 1990's, the dominant myth among conservatives was racial inequality no longer existed in modern-day America. Many believed education and income disparity existed, in part, because Blacks failed to take advantage of self-help programs like Project Head Start. As the dominant culture, many also believed they were in control and problems of inequality simply wasted away.

As a result, the Republican Party issued a declaration that year stating they spent forty trillion dollars in the fight for racial equality. Republicans also said citizens were living in a post-racial age of American democracy. The day after the declaration was issued, James Byrd, Jr., an African American man from Jasper, Texas was shackled in chains and dragged to his death by three White supremacists, all of whom he knew. In short, the state of relations for many people is a direct reflection and sign of a nation that's by no means self-possessed or free from racist agitation.

Situations that cause problems between the larger society and smaller cultural groups usually accounts for a small aspect of life events! In this way, no one situation highlights the complexity of relationships Blacks endure when living in America. Curiously, conservatives believe problems develop precisely because Black people lack ambition and fail to take advantage of opportunities. However, the problem with this unique theory is, up until recently, Whites made continuous efforts to oppress Black people.

America's past involvement includes slavery, the system of segregation, and discrimination against virtually every minority group arriving at America's great shores. So, Whites support for equality today may be lip service. In this way, behind closed doors, Whites may still harbor racist feelings toward them. In this case, Blacks have greater difficulty reaching full equality, especially in male dominant White society.

Still, there is a tertiary explanation, one perceived long ago by immigrant families, political refugees, and other minorities. If their values and statuses exist in the context of racial equality, then does not social injustice found in America reflect conformity with some aesthetic standard of correctness or propriety?

For instance, Congress condemns all ideas of divergence among cultural groups. Why? Racial inequality and social injustice seems to confirm White supremacy. Yet, the Ku Klux Klan believes its organization is free of corruption and immorality. How so? It operates under the constitutional right of free speech and right to bear arms in order to resist racial integration (change). In this way, Congress makes White supremacy the norm, contradicting certain beliefs or assumptions about White morality.

Many groups seek to resolve the problem of racial inequality. As a result, Whites show much more accepting attitudes toward minorities than fifty years ago. Although Whites tried to dispossess entire races in the past, the vast majority now support minorities in their fight for equal and greater opportunities. Racial violence, often perpetrated by Whites, diminished considerably thanks to earlier strategies and tactics used in the United States and other countries. Such methods involved nonviolent disobedience, political mobilization of resources, and moral suasion to mobilize public opinion. Curiously, some researchers question whether conservatives in White America will continue to move forward toward liberal racial attitudes or resist further change.

Social resistance often occurs when upwardly mobile Black families attempt to penetrate historically White neighborhoods. In the 1950's and 1960's, for instance, White parents pledged to resist racial equality; their children protested against school desegregation; and, the Klan opposed integration by carrying out mob violence and open attacks that represented more drastic measures of resisting Blacks and their families. However, their resilience taught Black people a lot about coping and surviving in the face of overwhelming adversity.

Nowadays, racism appears to be under control, reduced by government legislation. Yet, while Whites claim to be free of historical racism, racial prejudice and discrimination seem to have replaced it. As more Blacks struggle to reach equal status among Whites, they continue to be met with resistance.

Blacks intuitively understand that racial inequality comes from resistance. Those who are forced to play out various roles through their ascribed identity may find it more difficult to reach racial equality in the larger society. The problem worsens when the values, morals, and behavioral patterns of Black people differ from members in the larger society.

At the same time, belonging to a group in which one is highly valued can buffer the negative effects of stress and racial inequality. Unfortunately, there is no proof to indicate or suggest acceptance within a cultural group will translate into prestige among peers in dominant White society. Although membership among Blacks can raise esteem about one's ascribed identity, the person may still be met with strong opposition beyond the community. In this way, White discomfort, uneasiness, and fear continue to cause stress for Black people. However, we are only beginning to learn people can become members of more than one group, simultaneously, much like being ethnic and Caucasian, Buddhist and female, or gay and a church member. Although, being gay and a church member can create further difficulties for someone who is, per se, Christian.

The situation is bad for a man. Why? Gay men often reject the masculine role of male. In addition, their social status becomes of lesser value to the church while they are penalized by members of their own race for assuming a taboo role. In this way, their social role does not allow for a continually evolving and emerging identity. The result is gay males, like other minorities, will seek out membership in multiple peer groups.

In addition, some researchers believe one's social role varies across groups. An arousing extension of this view is whether *double jeopardy* exists for people who are minorities and members of a particular group. In this way, their position may not be socially acceptable, placing them at further disadvantage. For instance, being a Muslim American who votes Republican during a time he or she is living in America often proposes a problem for conservatives. Thus conservatives often have a strong, conscious need to discriminate against any cultural group or its members whose position may differ on valued dimensions.

Blacks are perceived to be doubly jeopardized as they suffer throughout their lifetime. For instance, they have very low social status in society from economic and social indignities caused by racial inequality. Their position becomes apparent as they mature throughout the lifespan. If they are Black and female, some would say their position appears to severely disadvantage them.

Yet, what's remarkable about Black people is their resilience and adaptation shown over the centuries. In a paternalistic society, Blacks developed their own social structures: community support systems to include Black churches, Black American kin systems, recreational bands and community associations, Black American family associations, and historically Black educational institutions, just to name a few. Blacks learned to master two cultures and have developed impressive strategies for adapting to life in America. Essentially, they learned to negotiate with dominant White society. Today, Blacks have their own social structures. Unfortunately, such interaction threatens the fundamental basis of racial equality.

"The Afro-Americanization of White youth," a term coined by Dr. Cornel West in his 1993-1994 book *"Race Matters,"* also called cultural appropriation, is taking its toll on conservatives in mainstream culture. The problem is young White males and females are emulating Blacks in their cultural styles of dress, attitude and behavior, and vernacular patterns of speech.

Amandla Stenberg (2015), a star in the movie "The Hunger Games," accused Kylie Jenner of appropriating Black features. Jenner wore her hair in cornrolls, a style of braids strongly associated with Black women around the world. In so many words, Amandla said Jenner was embracing Black hair styles. Yet, she refused to use her celebrity status to help up heave Black people from oppression.

Curiously, conservatives criticize cultural appropriation due to its mounting influence on core White values and cultural expectations. In this case, it is an objective condition of racial inequality they would like to change. How come? It affects some functional dimension of culture. What's ironic about cultural appropriation or, in this case, being Black when convenient is even though it's largely regarded as problematic, Whites who emulate Black people have greatly influenced change in mainstream thinking.

With racial tensions high between cultural systems, how can Black people buffer stress between Whites and themselves? Indeed, many Whites are hopelessly ensnared in racism, violent social behavior even. On the other hand, Blacks appear to be obsessed with gaining social status in dominant White society. These conflict differences leave little hope for resolution. Paradoxically, the way in which Whites learn to cope may differ from Black people.

White people built America on racist assumptions. Through their bigoted beliefs and opinions, which limit their thinking, they continue to demonize and demoralize

Black people. Such denigration is carried out through irrational feelings of discomfort, uneasiness, and fear. Yet, we are accustomed to thinking of America as a melting pot of cultures. So, how can Black people buffer the stress in their lives?

Better communication is perhaps the best way to reduce stress between the larger society and Blacks in America. In this way, both groups can reach an understanding without interpreting it as an unreasonable attempt to show supremacy or a manipulative effort to gain in social status. In addition, we may occasionally need to educate White families about the plight of Blacks in America. We may also have to educate them about certain difficulties Blacks might encounter in trying to gain rights to public access and important accommodations like fair housing. In this way, incidents that continue to cause racial inequality and social injustice will diminish considerably and positive interactions can begin.

It is also important to provide a better understanding of social norms and cultural expectations. Here, we may need to acknowledge certain strengths among Whites, such as pride in being White and Christian as well as take into consideration vulnerabilities like the impact of racial integration, same-sex marriage, and school desegregation, liberal attitudes that may make them feel victimized.

If the problem is a White and Black relationship, for instance, we might recommend they make compromises and concessions to the point that a positive impact occurs for both groups. The problem, then, may not be about individual differences or disliking someone due to racial characteristics, but dissimilarities between ethnicity and culture. Even so, both groups can make adjustments.

For instance, one group can learn to be more sociable. Or, its members can begin to communicate good intentions to the other group at the slightest hesitance of interaction. The other group, that which is unaccustomed to communicating with outside groups, can learn people who reach out are not necessarily trying to compete against them more than they are making an effort to be good neighbors. In this way, open communication facilitates learning and reasoning while reducing negative feelings of competition. The result is increased cooperative relations between them. Such relations will have a positive impact on the collective minds of community members.

However, conservatives in White America continue to carry over their heads the dark cloud of conflict. They also have little faith in those who do not conform to normative expectations. Conservatives and their critical acceptance of degrading ideals call into question the competency, capability, and possibility of Black people. These problems not only reinforce White hatred of minorities, but also make powerless their efforts to bring about the nature of their utopian hopes. Thus, they always consider Black people as having morally objectionable behavior.

This bourgeois mentality causes them to ignore the rich diversity and complexity of Black people. As a result, acculturating Blacks often distort and devalue their true nature in an attempt to win White peer approval. For them, stress is caused by conflict, which they create in trying to conform to social standards and the conventions of middle-class White Americans. Bourgeois Blacks may even completely lose their sense of self by emulating what others want them to be.

In the process, the external demands of reality often conflicts with their intuitive understanding. The result is low self-concept and esteem. However, they can improve their adjustment by developing positive self-perceptions, not worrying so much about conforming to what others want, and increasing positive interactions in the world. How we adjust to the world around us is largely a matter of change.

Change adheres to what is ordinarily accepted in society. However, we must recognize not all people are motivated to change. Repression lies behind some of our motives, even though we are capable of changing and adapting without being influenced by strangers and others. For instance, we retain the ability to change and adapt throughout our lives. Yet, people sometimes repress these abilities just to protect themselves from new experiences in anticipation of some ill-defined misfortune.

Those who cannot repress these natural abilities will develop exaggerated feelings of inadequacy or an inferiority complex. They are more likely to feel ashamed of their negative feelings thus not want them to be exposed. So they often develop aversions or avoidance behavior. Avoidance behavior may contribute to a perception of powerlessness over time. Repression works to push unacceptable thoughts and emotions out of consciousness so each one becomes or remains in the unconscious mind. Perhaps, aversion occurs when people cannot push unacceptable libido impulses out of awareness and back into unconsciousness. In a word, to better understand conservatism, we need to place stronger emphasis on aversion, a concept that might open the door to new objections.

Discussions of White discomfort, uneasiness, and fear still come down to whether we, as a civilization, can develop cooperative relationships. If we are to enhance the quality of living on earth, people need to deemphasize personal goals that involve self-serving values like feeling good, personal distinction, and independence. Many limitations found in Western cultures, like the United States, have too great an emphasis placed on self-serving values, which causes social phobias like aversion, xenophobia, nihilism, and conservatism. Hence, we need to place a stronger emphasis on collectivity.

Investigating connectedness to others and group behavior enables us to place greater emphasis on cultural values that serve the people, like preserving integrity, interdependence of members, and harmonious relationships. Regardless of their social background, people need a positive sense of self and connectedness if they are going to enhance the quality of life on this planet.

In this way, Dr. Martin Luther King, Jr., DD, would say, despite our differences we, *"a great people..."* will have *"...injected new meaning and dignity into the veins of civilization,"* referring to Blacks in their quest for racial equality.

Understanding the way conservatives view racial inequality is a complex undertaking and merits special attention. Perhaps my current effort to address the topic, through a paradox, will impact readers as well as reduce pain and suffering not only for Black people, but help make less troubling certain anxieties that control conservatives in dominant White society.

Chapter 2
Language of the Unheard: The Baltimore Riots of 2015

It is not enough for me to stand before you tonight and condemn riots. It would be morally irresponsible for me to do that without, at the same time, condemning the contingent, intolerable conditions that exist in our society. These conditions are the things that cause individuals to feel that they have no other alternative than to engage in violent rebellions to get attention. And I must say tonight that a riot is the language of the unheard.

Dr. Martin Luther King, Jr. DD
Speaking Weeks Before His Assassination (1968)

The new millennium ushers in more worries and greater vexations for White Americans. In the past, White folk worried about potential rebellion from foreign powers. That was then. Today, as America grows more diverse, Whites worry that immigrant families, political refugees, and other minorities will become the next state of rebellious dissatisfaction for White people in the country.

The Boston Marathon bombing of 2013, conducted by Bosnian immigrants Dzhokhar and Tamerlan Tsarnaev, gives White America cause for concern. The influx of African, Latino, Asian, and other minority groups also increase concerns. Due to their discomfort, uneasiness, and inherent fear, Whites feel there is heightening concern that minor insurrections or civil unrest will become increasingly common. The result is many White people want minorities to be teased apart from mainstream culture rather than have them live in concert.

Perhaps not as obvious to many people today is the mounting tension building and hatred poor Black people have for law enforcement. Attitudes in the Black community developed for more than half a century. The problem is such attitudes result from lack of political identity needed to establish a voice. However, social media proved to be an invaluable method in providing a voice for poor Black people. It is being used as a recruitment tool to help them voice their concerns against civil rights violations. Countless protesters are being recruited to organize and participate in peace rallies, peace marches, open protests, et cetera. Unfortunately, as tensions build in the Black community, many White people worry that protesting will add volume to the problem of combating an already complex threat.

Many White people feel the public attention Blacks receive from protesting will encourage, if not incite, terrorism on American soil. Whites feel young Black males are at greater risk of being solicited as domestic terrorists by Muslim organizations. White people worry that terrorist organizations recruit young Black males who are dissatisfied with civil rights violations occurring in their community. They say terrorists use social media to help recruit troubled Black males as potential jihadists. They believe terrorists provide central times and locations not only to young Black males, but young troubled Whites, so they can intimidate and kill off American citizens. As an example, Whites point to a foiled terrorist plot that took place at a Garland, Texas event.

White people gathered at the Curtis Culwell Center in Garland, Texas to poke fun at controversial cartoons of the Muslim Prophet Mohammed. Isis, a widespread,

Muslim terrorist group, claimed responsibility for two Muslim gunmen who tried to surprise attack participators of the event. The two young guns, Nadir Soofi and Elton Simpson, are referred to as Al Khilafa soldiers. Hours before the shootout, Elton Simpson posted a tweet on Twitter saying, *"May Allah accept us as mujahedeen,"* a term referring to Islamic fighters engaged in the struggle.

There is no question in the minds of many people that fifty years of racial prejudice and discrimination increased the complexity of attitudes found in the Black community. In fact, with certain injustices continuing in the Black community, many believe that Black people's attitudes are more complex than just a decade earlier. And now that there is the potential of domestic threats arising in urban areas, police commissioners work frantically to militarize their police force.

In contrast, President Obama vetoed bills used to provide police departments the right to militarize their police force through government assistance. But why are so many poor Black people unsupportive of law enforcement? After all, community relations should stabilize with more Blacks joining the ranks as police officer.

Many Black people believe Blacks who join law enforcement dismiss their moral obligations to race. Untold legacies of hatred found over the years suggest tensions are high as a result. In fact, tensions are more profound than what characterizes American racism.

Baltimore City Police Commissioner Anthony Batts was one of many Black police officers who people feel dismissed his moral obligations. People found Chief Batts' decision to stand in support of Mayor Stephanie Rawlings-Blake to be an extension of his dismissive attitude. He endorsed the Mayor even after she wrongfully stood in support of police officers whose actions were negligent and responsible for inciting the Baltimore riots.

When Mayor Rawlings-Blake condemned rioting in Baltimore as a disruption resulting from the actions of lawless criminals and thugs, people felt she dismissed her moral obligations to race. But what influences the attitudes of poor Black people? Attitudes develop when Blacks learn America is more than willing to exploit, oppress, and humiliate them. Racial profiling is one method police use to exploit, oppress, and humiliate Black people.

Operation Pipeline was a joint task force that used law enforcement officers to profile Jamaicans and Hispanics as a standard practice. Law enforcement profiled and arrested Jamaicans and Hispanics who traveled together along the New Jersey Turnpike. The belief was Jamaicans and Hispanics had common attributes likely to engage in criminal activity or any offense regardless of genuineness. Therefore, the two traveling together could be stopped and detained on suspicion of criminal wrongdoing.

Operation Pipeline led to the false arrest and wrongful conviction of countless Jamaican and Hispanic Americans. The Department of Justice describes *racial profiling* as any action used by the police that discriminates against a racial group, ethnic group, or national citizen with extreme prejudice not consistent with the probability of suspicious behavior. More humiliating offenses committed by law enforcement include symbolic forms of lynching. A symbolic lynching is exploitive, oppressive, and humiliating, not only to the person detained, but to community residents. Many residents experience overwhelming helplessness as a reminder of what could happen to them.

Those impoverished often express their feelings of hope for Black people who join law enforcement. After all, they do understand there is nobility involved in such a commitment. But, therein lays the problem. As law enforcement, police officers possess more acknowledged privileges than most other social classes in society. Along with the adoption of police values, customs, and traditions, they are taught to look down on poor Black people.

The surmounting misuse of police force, not only in White police abuse of authority, but usurpation of police authority by Black officers, and against Black citizens, serves as an example. The abuse and murder of Oscar Grant on January 1, 2009 by BART police officer Johannes Mehserle, when the situation did not warrant it, is another example. Unfortunately, White police abuse of authority is a continuing problem in urban cities across America. Black police abuse of authority has been problematic for some time.

Blacks in the United States find continuous interaction with police stressful. Many learn from years of police abuse and racial profiling that police officers are not very receptive to Blacks. They believe discord and discrimination are inevitable when law abiding citizens attempt to go about their daily lives. In addition, they feel marginalization imposes considerable stress on poor Black people and their families.

Many face chronic living conditions due to substandard housing, poverty, crime ridden and drug induced neighborhoods, burdensome responsibilities, and economic problems. Yet, they highly value neighborhoods and communities in which they live; they work to empower each other; and, they adhere to the American work ethic. Still, many Black people are hampered by police officers due to their minority status.

Poor Black people living in urban areas are harassed by the police department. Police harassment creates continued and unwanted annoyance on the part of law enforcement. Threats of false arrests, unrealistic demands, and police brutality create tensions.

Hostility emerges when wrongful arrests are made; arrests for suspicion of criminal mischief result in wrongful deaths against young Blacks; derogatory language and brute force are used to control innocent bystanders; and, complaints about the police go unheard, just to name a few potent stressors in the lives of poor Black people. Outraged citizens spur protests that often escalate into violence against police authority. Rioting results in looting, arson, and vandalism. Thus, for a people to go unseen and their voice unheard in the United States undoubtedly increases concern, and for all Americans.

News of White police abuse of Black Americans shocked a nation in denial. New York and Ferguson, Missouri would be the first cities to gain national attention from it. But what happened in Baltimore, Maryland would change the dynamics of intergroup relations, and how Whites would react to Blacks.

Network media released news about the amount of Blacks who died in police custody. Since 1999, the wrongful deaths of Eric Garner, Tamir Rice, Michael Brown, and a laundry list of many more Blacks across America to include Black women who were killed while in police custody, sparked outrage. As a result, on April 27, 2015, groups of High school students from all over Baltimore, Maryland rallied against local law enforcement.

Their protest was organized in an effort to stop police violence against Black citizens. The protest, which was meant to be a peaceful demonstration, served to defend the wrongful death of a young Black male named Freddie Grey (a twenty-five year old Baltimorean who died from injuries sustained while in police custody). The protest turned violent after the demonstration ended.

Officers took offense at students for protesting against police violence. Police then refused to allow students to ride city buses home. They sprayed students with mace and forbade bus drivers to seat them. Students retaliated against law enforcement officers. Students then converged on a police booth (located at Mondawmin Mall), pelted officers with rocks and bottles, set fire to police cruisers, and burned down buildings in retaliation against the misuse and abuse of police authority. American slavery, racial segregation, and a systemic society focused solely on the exploitation and oppression of Black people, proved to be too great a burden for many.

Young Blacks who were tired of being abused felt it was time to defend themselves against human rights violations, unfair treatment, and other unjust acts committed by local law enforcement. The irony was that many police officers who students pelted were Black. As Dr. Martin Luther King, Jr., DD would say, just when community relations appeared to change for the better, Baltimore's riots devastated a country. And the unheard spoke to White America in the only language they knew.

Community-based leaders express two theoretical views on the matter. The first view, supported by some leaders in the Black community, argues White police abuse of authority is the reason for mounting tensions occurring between law enforcement and Black citizens. They believe racism is the underlying problem. The second viewpoint, held by leaders who feel it's not about race, appeal their position to class and economic disparity.

They point out that many officers are taught to look down on Black citizens due to differences in their socioeconomic status. Not because of race! They feel that learning to cope with certain difficulties of lower income Blacks can lead to an exaggerated respect for Whites following the belief and opinion Whites do not exacerbate their disadvantages with problems of oppression, unemployment, poverty, and other states of hardship based on relative deprivation. They also understand that many Blacks in law enforcement learn to look down on those regarded as inferior.

They say that many Blacks, not just those in law enforcement, are under the impression Whites have better housing, nutrition, more wealth, and adequate healthcare for their children and themselves. In addition, many Blacks are conditioned to believe the average White person is more complex and better educated than themselves.

In contrast, while a few Whites may have professional careers in managerial positions or competitive occupations, many others do not. However, these individuals are not assigned to the same cultural stereotypes that typify Blacks in America or abroad. Ironically, the identity and life course perspective of many Blacks in law enforcement signify the intellectual experiences of people who have deluded feelings about supremacy.

Further, they say lost financial resources and poor social skills help to widen disparities. Being socially and economically disadvantaged, an overwhelming amount of Black Americans live in poverty or rank among the disproportionately poor. As evident, we find many Black families among the insufficiently educated. Illiteracy among Blacks is at an all time high in the United States. On average, 50% of Black Americans in urban areas drop out of school.

In contrast, White Americans are graduating at a rate 50% higher compared to their counterparts with the same academic abilities, especially in high-income and middle-income areas. Coupled with inadequate housing, dangerous neighborhoods, burdensome responsibilities, and economic uncertainties, chronic living conditions often dictate how White Americans perceive Black people. In this way, marginalization imposes considerable stress on poor Black people and their families. These statistics call for a serious sociocultural explanation. In brief, might fear of Black morality be explained by the fact race continues to be viewed as a measure of intelligence in Western culture?

Although Whites charge poverty among Black people comes from their failure to adapt or fit in, a minute few believed institutions could still play a greater role in helping to correct these cultural discrepancies. They believed if poor Black people were given better opportunities, it would provide them with a greater chance to progress. They wanted the US Government to provide poor Blacks with greater financial opportunity and more community resources to better accommodate them. But, what leaders of the latter viewpoint failed to consider was critical.

Black leaders who emphasize race most certainly agree various dimensions of culture disadvantage Black Americans. They say class and economic disparity are indisputable facts of the Black experience. However, while these community leaders acknowledge their argument is not the sole problem, they want people to understand there is a racial hierarchy in place.

Race-oriented community leaders criticize other community leaders for not understanding their point. They assert that the social stratification system was established by the cultural elite to legitimize White male patrilineal inheritance. It was put into place to give priority to or restrict inheritance of America to their White male offspring. As a result, only White males are born having filial rights and obligations to property, titles, equity, et cetera. In this way, our social system, which is stratified by class and economics, serves only to disadvantage Blacks and other minorities.

They further say the cultural elite masquerades under the ideology of free market capitalism. The cultural elite put people under the false assumption that capitalism is a system based on morals more than economics and politics. In this way, Blacks need to be morally right (truthful) or valid (useful) before Whites can properly assimilate them into the mainstay of American life. For Whites, the upward mobility of Black people depends on how well they can adhere to the American work ethic. In this way, conservative views reinforce racial hierarchies.

Race-oriented community leaders also point out that systemic problems in society are methods of institutionalized racism, a psychology and product of Western civilization. The method, they say, was uncovered by civil rights activist Stokely Carmichael and political scientist Charles Hamilton who coined the term in the 1960's. They remind people that institutionalized racism uses social exclusion to disadvantage Black people from certain entitlements of institutions.

Further, they pointed out that with institutionalized racism, there does not have to be any reasonable intention for certain racial groups to benefit or be disadvantaged. The intent is intertwined and mutually exclusive with the training and doctrine of many institutional policies. Housing agreements and loan policies along with barriers to employment and upward mobility are examples. Its structure, the arrangement and relations between parts of governing bodies, is what makes institutionalized racism the most dangerous, oppressive dimension.

Further, they want people to understand that our class-based social system is responsible for Black people internalizing racism. They say Blacks who have an exaggerated respect for their oppressor (and those who learn to look down on their own people) internalize racism. They emphasize that the internalization of racist attitudes is one reason community relations between Blacks in law enforcement and Black citizens are poor.

Internalized racism is a syndrome of hate that develops through exposure to traumatic events (like slavery or apartheid), severely oppressive situations (like in the case of poverty or prison), severe abuse (as in rape or police brutality), natural disasters (Hurricane Katrina, for example), or accidental disasters (like the Rockefeller coal-mining catastrophe in West Virginia, per se).

Internalized racism is largely identified as a suffering from degrees of hatred inflicted on a person through self-actions. Self-hatred can manifest through either a conscious or subconscious assimilation of bigoted beliefs or racist actions. In this case, an individual will adopt a racist attitude toward his or her own people, including themselves. He or she will begin to reinforce cultural stereotypes about his or her people and themselves. And, the individual will show aggression toward his or her people due to conscious or subconscious feelings of inferiority, imposed by an oppressor.

Anxiety symptoms like self-defeating thoughts, self-fulfilling prophecy, self-abuse, self-betrayal for which dependent males often manifest through a display of aggression in an exaggerated effort to retain self-control, are conditions that immediately follow self-hatred or delay symptoms by months, years even.

Indubitably, leaders who support the racial argument would like people to face the harsh reality that Blacks and other minorities often take on the social roles of their oppressors. Why are minorities so accommodating? Whites put a premium on their lifestyles. Mainstream living requires that Black people accept suffering while they accommodate White people in exploitative and oppressive ways.

In this way, accommodating Whites will prevent Blacks from changing the prevailing current of thought. It also keeps Black people from developing activities that would bring about an overthrow to the United States and its oppressive government. Only Blacks who are considered to be modeled citizens will benefit, especially those who dismiss their moral obligations to race. In addition, leaders assert that acculturating Blacks will have to abandon their morals if they are to have any chance of benefitting from interacting with mainstream culture.

Leaders who argue race also want people to know Blacks learned to survive and flourish despite the fact Whites tried to enslave or dispossess them in the past. Their resilience and adaptation led to the development of their own communities and social structures. They have Black churches, Black owned businesses, historically Black educational institutions, and many more important community resources help them to combat stress and oppression from the unfair demands and discriminative treatment of dominant Whites in America. In addition, they learned to negotiate with dominant White society. They also have a strong value system and great sense of community. Further, Blacks master strategies to help bring them into the mainstay of American life.

Finally, leaders who emphasize race conclude their argument by saying it is the wealthiest and richest Whites who create disadvantages for Black people. They say rich and wealthy Whites in America fear their lifestyle will be affected if they restructure programs to reflect the changing tapestry of today's society. They also say Whites still show resistance toward developing programs that would help poor Blacks reach full equality.

Resistance against affirmative action and school desegregation are two examples just to name a few. Whites are also reluctant to become involved in healthcare programs that may require tax cuts, affecting the rich and wealthy. Here, they play the old racial card to maintain control. Such resistance enables them to displace blame on Black people for continued problems the US Government allowed to build decades earlier. In this way, class and economic disparities are caused by Whites who hide behind tradition and institution to resist change.

In contrast, White people claim Blacks will not take advantage of opportunities other minorities are simply willing to consider. Their observations often follow inexperience in which case Whites draw inappropriate attention to Blacks by making vulgar remarks about them. Their nasty comments, combined with proud, self-serving remarks, more often lead them to legitimize discrimination against Black people. Even when Blacks attempted to seek out their fair share in housing, education, and employment markets, Whites continue to discriminate. Once racial tension and hostility emerge, requiring a resolution as it often does, Whites dismiss the minority viewpoint, and relations destabilize.

Recently, thousands of middle-class White Americans became part of the homeless population. The new homeless argue, vehemently, they are not the 1%. They say the 1% of Americans, who are the richest, has too great an influence over how our nation's consciousness is shaped. The new homeless also say it is no coincidence that from the superrich comes most of the president's cabinet and top ambassadors.

Whites argue that the new homeless are examples of what happens when rich and wealthy people attempt to accommodate minorities and their changing lifestyles. It

103

causes radical change and creates greater financial problems for White people. Other disadvantages are specific to certain ideas of culture.

Cultural barriers reflect differing views regarding what changes in values should occur and how each should be made. For instance, some Whites worry that differences in religion affect intergroup relations. Depending on the type of acculturation some Blacks receive in America, they will convert to Islam. Blacks who convert are not expected to remain Christian. But, generally speaking, religious differences will cause people to minimize social contact with one another.

In another instance, Islamic people believe the wearing of Christian crosses is blasphemy, expressing disrespect for Allah and their sacred way of life. In this way, they are accused of teaching intolerance and religious indifference while instilling the Islamic faith in their children. Other differences, like behavior patterns, beliefs, social customs, history, dress, diet, and even kin systems people used to help them cope with stress, results in more displaced aggression for Whites.

Today, White police abuse of authority continues to spark occasional incidents of conflict and hatred between Whites and Blacks. Black leaders believe class and economic disparity factors into police abuse. Health, wealth, and income disparity create indifferences that place poor Black people on unequal footing with the larger dominant society. And as a reiteration: It enables White people to displace blame on Blacks for continued problems the US Government allowed to build decades earlier.

In this way, it is easy to understand how class and economics factor into the thinking strategies of White police officers. We further gain a better understanding of why or how so many Black police officers chose to abuse their authority. In this way, it becomes clear why internalized racism needs to be taken into careful consideration. Such consideration betters community relations.

There is a placid acceptance among Americans that characterizes denial. We as a nation are unwilling to consider challenges that allow for the upward mobility of Blacks. The vast majority of people tolerate interracial tensions while Whites continue to exert considerable pressure on Blacks and their families.

Despite certain beliefs, denial will cost each and every person access to the American dream. We already started off the new millennium on a wrong note. Despite progress toward gender identity, discrimination, and a declining economy, we refuse to overcome the great divide; we fail to fight against poverty; and, we deny minorities their rights to access. In this way, Whites use strangers and others to buffer the impact of continued problems between Whites and Blacks (historical issues allowed to build for decades). Acculturating minorities fail to have discussions on issues that affect the daily lives of their poor. They lack the courage necessary to challenge established authority and institutions. Meanwhile, liberal Whites, Black Democrats, and poor Black people fail to confront certain truths about a declining economy and cultural decay consuming them.

As a result, their needs more often go unmet. As Dr. Cornel West said in his national best seller, <u>Race Matters</u> (1993-1994):

> ...we seem to lack the patience, courage, and hope necessary to reconstruct public life—the very lifeblood of any democracy.

My goal in this chapter was not to blame Whites for showing a less than acceptable attitude toward Blacks. Nor was it my intentions to criticize them for the rare and usually short-lived moments we work to improve the lives of one another. But, when White people dismiss the concerns of Black people as a problem of triable ignorance, differences are incorrectly assumed, and that indifference leads to further disadvantages.

Certainly, we need to look at cultural decay in the Black community. But, we also need to condemn any heathenish acts that contribute to incorrect assumptions about the values of Blacks, Asians, and other minorities. Last, we must look at the circumstances in which people are born and raised. In doing so, we begin to meet the immediate needs of people who are affected by their circumstances.

In fact, my goal is to inform and educate society about its adherents, people who set group norms. I may not be able to exert change through normative influence as a minority. But, if my views are presented consistently and confidently, each will provide new opportunity to critique a society that exerts both normative and informational pressure on Black people.

My views may also show Blacks are able to cause dissent. I can then show disagreement is possible and Black people are able to influence those who participate in the decision-making of fundamental institutions that hold sway over them. Therefore, White Americans will more likely listen to the views of Blacks as the best course. Certainly, many critics believe certain Black people play a key role. However, they believe Blacks must work through informational pressure.

Can Blacks win against the majority in that way? There will be occasions when they have their day once committed to do so.

During the Civil Rights era, when racial segregation and social injustice dominated and racism tore at the very fabric of American democracy, Dr. Martin Luther King, Jr., DD, aided Black Americans in establishing important rights. Before that, Malcolm X and his Black Nationalist viewpoints helped awaken Black people from their captivity to the tragic reality of White male supremacy. So it goes without saying, the method minorities use to convince a cultural majority determines the circumstances that affect life chances for everyday, ordinary people.

Chapter 3
Biracialism in America

Seeking an identity is about trying on one face after another, looking for one's own.

Allen and Santrock,
Psychology: The Context of Behavior (1993)

Many cultures walk along these great shores and, in the exchange of cultural values, often mix beliefs and identities. Some lose their identity. Others retain certain elements of it. Still, there are those who will be absorbed into an established mainstream only to emerge with new identities. As identity lines begin to blur, one thing becomes clear. New prospects for these changing faces are unclear.

Recent discussions regarding multiculturalism in America—especially a propos intermix of racial and ethnic groups—raise important questions about new prospects for biracialism in America. Two schools of thought express views on this topic. However, there is dissension among members of the first school. Dissenters' argument involves the notion that biracial Americans may have no interest in promoting Western customs and traditions. In this way, they believe having a dual heritage will prevent them from becoming an integral part of the larger society. We call these dissenters conservative.

On the other hand, there are those who believe the larger society will work as a constraint of life chance for biracial Americans. Their viewpoint argues, although the larger society shows a much more accepting attitude toward people with dual heritages, today's society is still cruel and its members will cause them to endure a psychology of victimization. Coupled with certain insecurities most conservatives have about intermixing, society will force biracial people to find alternative lifestyles.

Others will seek out interaction with multiple peer-groups just to avoid undergoing unpleasant or undesirable circumstances. Those who consent to this viewpoint are in agreement with members from the second school of thought. We readily call these consenters liberal, a term used interchangeably with Republicans and Democrats.

Conservatives, those who follow tradition as an institution, believe as identity lines blur, biracial Americans will lose interest in promoting long-established customs and beliefs. For instance, they feel biracial Americans will not maintain established authority and institutions meant to keep America in the tradition of Western culture. On the other hand, liberals believe biracial Americans will be adversely affected by hate crimes and alienated just like those in the past.

Democrats recently called for the mandate of anti-hate crime laws. Their reason for the mandate is to ensure minorities like women, lesbians, gays, Blacks, people from different social backgrounds, and those with dual heritage, will no longer endure hardship. In a capsule, the future for biracial Americans largely depends on fundamental challenges that force change in how society interacts with them.

Unfortunately, these two schools haven't done nearly enough to elevate the racial debate for biracials.

Such a debate should take place about new prospects for biracialism in America. This debate must move far beyond the reaching point, breaking cultural expectations in three fundamental ways. First, both schools must come to understand racism and psychology go hand-in-hand with tradition and institution in which case each concept is interchangeable. Institutions are so long-established and universal each one set the priority cultures value as a tradition. Such priority sets the circumstances that biracial Americans often endure. However, we can change their circumstances through simple means of adjustment.

Next, both schools must come to understand culture is more than behaviors associated with an ethnic group. Culture is rooted in traditions that define our institutions. Churches, schools, music, and network social media like television, radio, and now the Internet come from long-established customs and beliefs by which we aspire even though the Internet may help to blur identity lines for those who use it.

Each one promotes a psychology of concepts handed down from generation-to-generation. Institutions are influenced by culture and ethnicity and are viewed as a set of precedents. Culture is also necessary to conduct healthy intergroup relations. It determines how people or ethnic groups behave or how nature, reality, or events are perceived.

Last, and most important, both schools must be willing to unravel certain problems biracial Americans endure at the hands of the large society. For a biracial

American caught up between two worldviews, problems they confront speak volumes. The psychology of victimization for a biracial is caused by people who contribute to an attenuation of those whose appearance may not reflect accepted standards of the larger society. Rather, their appearance may reflect the aesthetic nature of a diverse and enriched ethnic group.

This analysis is not in any way to say people with dual heritages do not discriminate. Many do and often against members of the rejected half of their dual heritage. In fact, biracial people reject their own all of the time. But, biracial forms of discrimination more often comes from a people who want no further conflict in their lives. Biracials are especially resistant to people who may upset the status quo. To talk about the effects of low esteem that comes from discrimination, withdrawal, isolation from peers and family, or losing themselves in a crowd, is problematic in and of itself. But, to own up to punishing a biracial—just because his or her dual heritage is perceived to be in violation of cultural expectations—requires further consideration.

Conservatives describe American culture as a homogeneous melting pot. So, the problem becomes apparent rather than actual for them. Conservatives tend to have negative thinking strategies and fail to understand the rich diversity of having a dual heritage. Why? They fail to consider diverse cultural groups as a part of the American process. America is greatly influenced by traditions that are rooted in Greek and Roman culture as well as Christianity.

All other cultures and traditions that develop, in their mind, is purely a failure to adapt, and part of society that does not reflect Western customs and beliefs.

The problem with both schools is each one lacks the courage necessary to discuss America, a diverse and multicultural society. A series of historical, economical, and social experiences produced this bold and beautiful nation of ours. The result is America produced many cultures, swarming with different customs, family structures, and languages. Although their failure to adapt no longer benefits the growth and prosperity of Western culture, conservatives continue to show dissent by discouraging cultural differences.

Other countries may differ from our own. But, we can develop a better understanding of biracialism by recognizing and respecting legitimate differences between us. However, if ever there was a taboo topic to discuss at the dinner table, it would be biracialism, the result of multiculturalism. Why? In doing so, many of us would be ridiculed in the same way closed-minded people berate Blacks in America. This problem is more so true due to our increasingly interdependent world, which is beginning to weigh in on the thinking strategies of White Americans.

Not many people can investigate into the thinking strategies of those who perceive biracial experiences as separate from their own. Those who can may want to see whether separatists have difficulty perceiving Western culture as a melting pot or multicultural society. They may find many people who dislike intermixing are not motivated by racism and racial discrimination at all. In fact, such a perception may essentially be motivated by a lack of education or information.

Similarly, people who perceive Western culture as a melting pot (and those who assimilate certain ideals to accommodate the larger society) cannot provide the stimulus necessary to effect change in one's thinking. What is often found among them is avoidance behavior. Avoidance behavior would indicate social separation is motivated by an irrational pattern of discomfort, uneasiness, and fear. In this case, aversions place people like conservatives at greater social distances from Blacks, Asians, gays and, yes, biracial Americans.

Conservatives are profoundly ethnocentric. They tend to judge biracial Americans solely by the values and standards relative to the rejected half of their dual heritage. That is to say, conservatives judge biracial Americans by whichever identity differs from their own. Since they tend to live in environments that do not intermix and have even less interaction, it is believed lack of exposure early on in the process of child development influence their unjust attitudes. For them, the perception of biracialism as a part of Western culture, as with other interpretations, is limited by their lack of exposure. As interpreted by people who do interact, multiculturalism (much like integration) encourages people from different racial, ethnic, and religious backgrounds to maintain cultural integrity while becoming an integral part of the larger society.

Moreover, biracialism will occur as a continuation of Western culture. This realization is true, whether conservatives choose to maintain their traditional way of life, even if they desire an independent existence, and even though its members continue to exercise their power to exclude people whose skin color and customs may, in some way, differ from their own (as in segregation). Such threats are not simply a matter of culture and institution though these structures are necessary for healthy intergroup relations. In fact, biracialism in America is a primary concern of people who fail to understand how two separate and distinct cultural systems can intermix. In this way, how can Americans begin to celebrate the rich diversity and common grounds shared if they cannot appreciate biracialism as a mutually enriching part of the American process?

Conservatives also discuss biracialism as if acknowledging skin color is unconscionable, hence the term color-blindness. On the surface, the notion of a color-blinded society may very well sound reasonable to many of us: judging someone by the content of their character not by the color of their skin appeals to many people today. But, short catchy phrases cannot remove the cascade of historical, economical, and social experiences that produced these differences between us. What's curious about this inspirational catchphrase (color-blindness) is the implication that conservatives are unable to adequately deal with diversity in broader cultural dimensions. In this way, their attempts to interact with people from diverse social backgrounds depend on how well they learn to ignore skin color.

While biracialism is hardly a shortfall, for too long, the larger society viewed virtually any difference in appearance a deficit. Too often, members of the larger society took advantage of these differences. They justified their own biases by exploiting, oppressing, or humiliating people from different social backgrounds. What's particularly ignorant and arrogant about Post-Party Conservatism is its members continue to define themselves in ways that hurt development toward more complete, modern social conditions. In this way, everything in its ignorant arrogance kills itself.

As for liberals, they not only have wrongful impressions about biracial Americans but inadvertently contribute to our poor perceptions of them: who they are, what they're all about, and their ambitions in life. But wait, that analysis is a serious indictment in need of clarification. Biracialism becomes especially stressful for those who just learned to cope with integration while the coming generation is beginning to intermix. A step in the wrong direction, some might say.

The intermixing of groups previously segregated caused so-called liberals to rethink their overall strategies. They are beginning to understand what conservatives in the past feared most. Some say integration will lead to the intermixing of groups, and a loss of identity would occur even for their people (the beginning of a perceived end). In this way, liberals also fear a considerable amount of confusion and anxiety for their people due to an exchange of cultural values. Still, some do understand that if minorities were to cooperate within the larger social system, while maintaining cultural integrity, neither group would lose essential features of their culture. In this way, no one group would be pressured to change its way of life. Essentially, the notion of racial and ethnic groups intermixing is, perhaps, the very reason why integration has yet to be fully realized.

Understanding this lively controversy, the debate about new prospects for biracialism in America, involves a psychology of victimization found to be increasingly common. Here, *victimization* refers to the lived experience of coping in a society that continues to socially exclude and persecute people due to differences in their heritage. In this way, discrimination is not a new practice in America.

Biracial Americans were born as a result of the absurd. The raping of enslaved African women by White slave Masters in America produced many children born with dual African and European heritage. Many times, having a dual heritage gave these children no peace of mind. Slave masters also victimized biracial children who made extraordinary efforts to overcome the enslaved circumstances of a world to which they rightfully belonged. According to an ad entitled "Raising Biracial Children to be Well Adjusted," written by author Nadra Kareem Nittle on About.com, it reads:

> *Biracial children have existed in the United States since colonial times. America's first child of dual*

African and European heritage was reportedly born in 1620. Despite the long history biracial children have in the U.S., opponents to interracial unions insist on invoking the tragic mulatto myth to justify their views. This myth suggests that biracial children will inevitably grow into tortured misfits angry that they fit into neither black nor white society. While mixed-race children certainly face challenges, raising well-adjusted biracial children is possible if parents are proactive and sensitive to their children's needs.

Curiously, the threat to biracial Americans is neither Western tradition nor hate crimes, but identity confusion that comes from experimenting with various roles in search of their own identity. So long as those who experiment with various social roles fail to find an identity of their own, they will remain in crisis and become confused. Here, *psychology of victimization* refers to the mental suffering biracial people endure to gain acceptance from a particular group that may be unnecessary for the emergence of a new identity.

Biracial Americans try to identify with members of the more mutually beneficial heritage. According to Nikki Khanna and Cathryn Johnson from Time.com, authors of an article entitled "Passing as Black: How Biracial Americans Choose Identity," they propose:

The practice of passing—identifying with and presenting oneself as one race while denying ancestry of another—reached its peak during the Jim Crow era... In the segregated landscape of the late 1800s and early 1900s, the "one-drop" rule labeled as black any person who had mixed blood.

Those with more white ancestry than black, and who therefore looked whiter, were the ones who tended to pass.

Still, many were and are rejected, devoid of membership and any hope for social development in broader cultural dimensions. According to the claims of conservatives, social rejection is not about deliberate exclusion from interaction for social reasons. Rather, social rejection of biracial Americans is a practical response by people who fail to consider matters and dealings perceived as other than their own. Here, we must recognize the psychology of victimization reflects differing concepts regarding what causes cultural differences and how others should be treated. However, the reality is such victimization fosters cultural problems, reinforces normative expectations and, quite frankly, becomes more prevalent as the larger society continues to be fortified against a people whose skin color and social customs may, in some way, reflect their own.

But why has this fortification taken root? Why do barriers continue to exist? There are two basic views about the existence of cultural barriers. On one side, there are those who value and praise progress made to remove cultural barriers. They believe significant strides were made during the civil rights era. They point to affirmative action programs as proof these advances exist.

On the other side are those who criticize affirmative action programs like Project Head Start and Upward Bound. They believe cultural barriers continue to characterize these institutions. We have made progress toward healthy intergroup relations; but, cultural barriers still exist; and, equality has yet to be achieved.

Knocking down old barriers in America is possible. But, much still needs to be considered. It is important to recognize cultural barriers are especially challenging in intergroup relations. Although it may appear insignificant to many, biracial Americans are often discriminated against in this way.

Like most minorities, the spectrum of living conditions and lifestyles for biracial Americans are influenced by social class, social and language skills, occupational opportunities, and social resources. Such a system of support can be compared to the availability of meaningful support networks we find in the extended family. Such a system of support may be especially important resources to improve their sense of self and help them to cope with their dual heritage.

Their dual heritage includes a broad diversity in national backgrounds and lifestyles. Such diversity ranges from highly acculturated biracial Americans who may be better educated than the average American to the unacculturated, lacking in financial resources and having poor social skills. Language can sometimes, but not often, be a barrier for an unacculturated biracial in daily interactions. Effective communication with neighbors, educators, and potential employers is challenging in that case.

Other barriers may be specific to certain cultures, reflecting cultural differences in ideas, values, and beliefs. For instance, cultural differences may prevent communication in ways that adversely affect Christians and Muslims. Race becomes a barrier for many others, especially when their occupation, wealth, education, and family status fail in comparison to members of the larger society. Prejudice and segregation are historical underpinnings for the psychology of victimization that adversely affects their lives in so many ways.

Cultural barriers to race also include workplace discrimination, housing discrimination, rights to access, and other forms of inequality. Curiously, biracial Americans are more often in denial about why the larger society refuses to accept them. They tend to be confused about their place in society. And, they tend to be upset with how others perceive them. Still, many feel a positive connectedness to members of the larger society. Apparently, the need to belong remains strong among them. Why so?

While biracial Americans show remarkable resilience and adaptation by exploring a number of roles, many reject characteristics that single them out as a minority. These characteristics are either devalued or repressed. For instance, a biracial may view their own values as undesirable and physical features a hindrance or disadvantage to the production of the larger society. Gradually, they may be compelled by an event that causes them to realize they will never be fully accepted in society.

That realization might be a rude awakening brought on by being bashed or discriminated against by the very people they come to consider as friends, peers, and acquaintances. Along with more identity shattering events people trigger later on in life, the biracial then begins to form an appreciation for the previously rejected half of his or her dual heritage. Last, the biracial later learns to appreciate the benefits of embracing both heritages.

Cultural barriers are also fraught with problems. Each one is full of distress, difficulties, and dangers. However, there are many forms of cultural barriers and each affects people in many domains of American life. Age, gender, and other barriers further separate people. Separation often prevents them from gaining important access. The realization works to emphasize differences in cultural beliefs.

Some people believe America is tolerant of biracial folk more than the typical minority. However, many biracial Americans continue to have important access denied. Why? In thinking about Western culture, the reason to deny a biracial access is for an underlying need to maintain supremacy.

What needs to change? In what way has society gone awry? Our communities and social structures include Black churches, Japanese language schools, Chinese American family associations, Vietnamese mutual assistance associations, Mexican American kin systems, Indian bands and tribal associations, and White fraternal and charitable organizations with rights to access and other privileges. Yet, not one of us can fully understand why structures meant to buffer stress for so many people fail to help biracial Americans develop strategies needed to cope and survive a psychology of victimization.

On the other hand, it could be the rise of hate groups in the 1980's and early 1990's, the reinstitution of American apartheid schools, poverty and discrimination throughout the new millennium, segregated communities (which continue to exist), or the cumulative impact of recessions, that play an important role in the everyday circumstances of each and every American. The answer to those questions is paradoxical in that it's more likely all of the above yet may not be one.

How do biracial Americans learn to cope? Searching for identity, biracial Americans experiment with various roles. Those who successfully explore a number of alternatives find their identity and thoughts become more conceptual and reasonable. Hence, they have considerably more control over how people perceive them. Nevertheless, there will be issues with love and hate that suggest a time of identity confusion. Such a paradox involves learning how to see one's dual heritage as mutually enriching.

The impotence of our society is we have no buffers to help biracial Americans cope with a psychology of victimization, to aid them in overcoming the stress of having two worldviews, rise above social rejection, minimize the effects of aversive racism, to knock down structural barriers like culture-bound and class-bound values, and removing language as a barrier. Social structures are built to help buffer the impact of severe stress and oppression. Each one reinforces community and wellness.

In other words, to help buffer the stress in their lives, we must help biracial Americans understand the importance of perceiving both heritages as mutually enriching. We can also accommodate them with social structures that reduce the psychology of victimization. In fact, how we learn to accommodate them can teach us much about ourselves. If, however, we cannot accommodate biracial Americans through our resilience and adaptation, then no one is to be applauded. For now, biracial Americans continue to experiment with one role after another in search of their own identity.

Chapter 4
The Plight and Predicament of Blacks in America

Yet, in familiar American fashion, genuine white peer acceptance still preoccupies—and often escapes—them. In this regard, they are still affected by white racism.

Cornel West,
Race Matters (1993)

As an African American, I am deeply disturbed by the plight and predicament of Blacks in America. Those at the bottom left of society appear to be in complete denial of all established authority and institutions. In contrast, conservative Blacks are a class of acculturating minorities who think in the mainstream. They often relinquish their cultural identity to better establish themselves in the larger society. This move is difficult, especially as they try to penetrate historically White communities. Paradoxically, what's ignoble about the woeful plight of both groups is their continued ability to survive a situation that results in complete denial of rights, privileges, and opportunities.

Poor Blacks believe their situation is the cause of severe stress and oppression. Slavery, segregation, poverty, discrimination, and poor education document the impact of chronic living conditions. Their situation is said to come from having lost cultural and psychological contact with both their traditional society and the larger dominant society. The results are feelings of alienation and identity loss. For those reasons, many are said to be disorganized and unsupportive of acculturating Blacks.

On the other hand, acculturating Blacks are often absorbed into an established mainstream; sometimes they may even merge to form an integral part of society. They offer themselves as examples of how well the system works for those who are not afraid to sacrifice and work hard. However, these emerging affluents are overly concerned with trying to establish their self. As a result, many relinquish their cultural identity. The loss of cultural identity is said to be a personal sacrifice that allows for a better exchange of cultural values. Yet, in the genuine spirit from which equality is and has always been admired, serious attempts to mainstream Blacks are often ignored, rejected even.

As acculturating Blacks attempt to penetrate historical White communities, interracial tensions mount. The result is they have greater difficulty reaching equality. Their situation is said to be further eroded by prejudice and discrimination. Discrimination affects our undifferentiated consciousness. In this way, our self-concept and esteem are negatively impacted by strong influences in the social environment; the psychological result is identity-confusion.

Prejudice causes contempt of self or self-hatred; one can note prejudice by paying careful attention to blatant forms of discrimination. Here, one can see prejudice directed at the targeted. Its impact is so undeniable some unfortunate person will often suffer from adverse circumstances. The group or member against whom Whites are prejudiced can be from a particular race, ethnicity, culture, nation, sex, age, religion, or some other notable characteristic. Both prejudice and discrimination are part of a social exclusion and persecution process meant to enforce racial supremacy in America.

Here, acculturating Blacks adapt their values and beliefs system to a bad situation. They struggle for acceptance. Still, they sacrifice and work hard to achieve it. Even so, what they refuse to understand is most Whites will never accept Black people on the basis of merit. Instead, they blame programs like Affirmative Action for their disadvantages.

They've come to believe that without Affirmative Action programs, White people will learn to accept them on the basis of merit rather than race. Yet, dominant White society gives them no reason to suspect its members would otherwise support acculturating Blacks in their wrongful conclusions. In this regard, they are in complete denial of their situation. They are in denial about Affirmative Action programs, most of which afford many opportunities into areas where Black people are simply unwanted. Still, they continue to support dominant White society and often to their detriment.

Consider how the conservative class of acculturating Blacks voted in the year 2012. Their psychological desire to seek out positive interactions with dominant White society is, in response, a blind loyalty to the nation. Supporting Republicans in their effort to elect former Speaker of the House, Newt Gingrich, entrepreneur Herman Cain and then, Governor Mitt Romney for US Presidency was an extreme move for any person who has conservative political views. Yet, conservative Blacks lend their support for Governor Romney even though he was considered a religious radical. Newt Gingrich's blunted theories about the posting of Black people in America were dated and offensive. Still, he was the conservative choice for Presidential Office. Now, let's discuss the tragicomic situation of incompetency displayed by Herman Cain. He allowed himself to be used as a symbolic gesture (court jester) on behalf of the Republican Party.

Ironically, many conservative Blacks supported his core principles. Not one Republican nominee was qualified to run for Presidential Office that year. Yet, in true ad hoc, faux pas fashion, Republicans presented their nominees as competent and qualified Representatives. However, words of approval seldom passed the lips of registered voters. Thus, Republicans wrongfully concluded the public could be bought on approval.

The problem started when Newt Gingrich failed to code racist language in a way that reflected everyday decorum. Conservative Whites then asked him to resign from the Presidential campaign. Having no favorable Representatives left, they simply made good use of a bad situation: They exploited Herman Cain. What's wrong with Herman Cain, you ask? He was a distraction used by conservatives in the Republican Party to undermine the potential talent of Black politicians. His nomination, a bold and daring move, did give them a big advantage, however. It allowed conservatives to showcase their nominees as the best qualified Representatives; they were not. Next, it served as a way to convince people Republicans were

132

trying to remove the shackles of mental colonialism from the minds of Americans; yet, they were not. Finally, it was a way to show the country conservative Whites were America's only real hope for restoring all established authority and institutions; still, they are not.

Yet, their diabolical game plan impacted Americans. How so do you ask? After two failed attempts by the Republican Party, Mitt Romney looked pretty good in the eyes of conservative voters. Allow me to further enlighten you on their mental reasoning. As said, conservative Whites feel threatened by the potential of intellectual talent found in Black leadership. Therefore, they develop strategies to help convince generations of registered voters not to take competent Black politicians seriously in future office elections. In this way, Herman Cain's incompetency (again, a distraction) would convince a new generation of conservative supporters to reject the idea of having another Black person serve as US President. As a result, competent and viable Black politicians, like Republican Representative Allen B. West, would not get his chance to prove himself amendable in the public eyes. What, in some people's minds, would be a real travesty (so I've heard).

The need for conservative Blacks to devote themselves in ways careless of political consequences as if there were no more competent and qualified Black Republican Representatives available in political office is for greater acceptance and respect from dominant Whites. Thus, their conservative position shows how hopelessly ensnared they are in their desire to gain White peer approval. Needless to say, Romney won the conservative Black vote in 2012.

Conservative values often cause emerging affluents to show contempt toward their own people. The problem is Blacks are perceived as burdensome to dominant Whites. They consider them to be flawed and impeded by performance and productivity in some way. Unhealthy conceptions put considerable pressure on Blacks to change. In turn, many acculturating Blacks adopt conservative values.

Conservatives then assimilate their ideals to better accommodate the larger society. Depending on the level of acculturation, many will develop contempt for their own people. They feel hindered by liberals who believe conservative Blacks owe an obligation to uplift a people they consider unfit by moral weakness. Many offer their apologies for the personal failings of poor Blacks. Here, they make distinctions between their intellectual processes as different.

The resultant justification is the alleviation of a burdensome responsibility that binds them to the Black community. That way, they can relinquish all cultural ties. For those reasons, liberals are frustrated by the value process of assimilation. Curiously, conservative Blacks are assimilated into the social system of mainstream society, which suggest they too are not well-adjusted to the mainstay of American life.

Liberals believe cultural assimilation causes Black people to undergo a considerable amount of confusion and anxiety. Instead, they offer a healthier adaptation to acculturative pressures. They offer integration as a way to maintain cultural integrity while cooperating within the larger social system. Integration has its benefits under certain circumstances even though it can be stressful for those who seek out assimilation. Through integration, however, poor Blacks can become an integral part of the larger society. Liberals encourage stronger support of community and wellness programs to strengthen unity among Blacks. Wellness programs are designed to achieve moral soundness among Black people. For this reason, Blacks who support assimilation do not believe in chastising dominant Whites for holding conservative beliefs. They feel liberals also refuse to be influenced by the pressures of change.

Conservative Blacks reject the idea of community and wellness. In this way, they reject their moral obligations to race. They believe poor Blacks lack strength of mind that enables them to endure adversity with courage and conviction. This fault, they believe, is one reason poor Black people fail in their efforts to survive the pressures of change. Further, they believe a failure of nerve from poor Blacks more often forces society to look at all Black people as victims.

Conservative Blacks believe poverty is no excuse nor is discrimination a sufficient reason for the insoluble attitudes apparent among poor Black people. For this reason, they relinquish their cultural ties to the Black community. Their hope is to gain mainstream acceptance for having the ability to produce solutions in some problem domain, not because some government program mandate Whites and Blacks interact. They argue that government mandated programs work only to reinforce unhealthy conceptions of Black people. Many feel race-free merit systems will ease racist perceptions of Black people in places like the American job market. For those reasons, they advocate the dismantling of Affirmative Action programs.

Ironically, people should understand Affirmative Action is a negative means to reaching equality. After all, it was put in place to ensure dominant Whites lose their inherent right to freely discriminate against women and other minorities. Although White women and men are its greatest benefactors, Black people continue to be unemployed at alarming rates, and Affirmative Action still contributes to racist perceptions in the workplace, without it, seeking out equal opportunities in the American job market will become an impossible obstacle to overcome.

Since we live in a society that has discriminated against virtually every racial group arriving at its shores, world cultures even, it is likely, without the mandate of Affirmative Action programs, discrimination will increase significantly. In places where the population is predominately White or from employment decisions that come down to favoritism, nepotism, and just plan ole American cynicism, race-free merit systems will result in complete denial of rights, privileges, and opportunities. In this way, poor Blacks consider their conservative counterparts to be out of touch with important constitutional changes in society.

In the past, poverty and discrimination translated to certain rights, privileges, and economic opportunities being withheld from minorities, specifically Black Americans. For instance, the Industrial Period, World War I, and the Great Depression marked out the beginnings of public assistance programs in America. It is my belief the government took this opportunity to enhance suffrage. For example, public service agencies began a campaign to remove the Black man from homes where women were receiving public assistance.

Agencies carried out this plan under the assertion Black men were shiftless, lazy, and would not adequately provide for their family in times of need. The result was more poverty, increased crime, prostitution, drug abuse, and higher dropout rates in grade schools for Black children. Poor housing opportunities, underemployment, unemployment, homelessness, and public handouts were also culprit in the persecution of young Black males. As well, Hispanics and other minorities were disadvantaged in this way.

Today, continuous recessions waged from wars are destroying the American economy. And, chronic living conditions help to typecast poor Black people as inherently weak, lazy, and incompetent. Since their situation reinforces certain beliefs, poor Blacks are often paid low wages and given menial jobs. Bank teller, secretary, and cashier are the most common means of employment for poor Black women. Poor Black men, on the other hand, can be found working as short-order cooks, postal workers, correction officers, and factory workers, if lucky.

In the United States, Canada, and the United Kingdom, jobs defined as menial employment too often have low pay, low status, and little security. The coming generation in North America call these means of earning income *ghetto jobs* or the practice of giving low paying employment opportunities to minorities. Until recently, only developing countries did not discriminate on the basis of skin color. However, many did practice giving good paying employment opportunities to family members, friends, and network associates.

Although whites no longer use blatant forms of discrimination to disadvantaged Black people, they adopt subtle ways to express their discontent. Too often, business employers minimize the hiring of minorities. The government often praise companies for sticking to their hiring policies. Meanwhile, the good-ole-boys network still manages to restrict employment opportunities and applications to in-house promotions and specific zip codes.

The present situation of Black people—an unpleasant combination of circumstances in which prejudice and segregation are historical underpinnings for the chronic stress of poverty and discrimination—adversely affects their health and wellness. Their situation occurs precisely because American life forces them to confront those tragic facts. In supporting the dismantling of government mandated programs, we recreate a situation where Black possibility cannot continue or occur. In this way, those who hastily reject Affirmative Action are in complete denial of their situation.

Fortunately, Black people now have their own communities and social structures to help buffer the severe stress of poverty and discrimination. Each cultural development shows remarkable resilience and adaptation for coping under chronic living conditions in America. Support systems like churches, family associations, and kin systems show the progressive efforts of those who overcome severe stress and oppression. There is even an increase in higher learning among poor Blacks despite having to endure chronic living conditions. As a result, many develop impressive strategies for negotiating with dominant White society. Curiously, acculturating Blacks turn their attention away from poor Blacks who learn to effectively cope with the situation of poverty.

Frequent characterization of poor Blacks as problematic is the prime reason why acculturating Blacks relinquish their cultural identity. In this way, they do not consider their own people to be victimized by the severe stress of poverty and discrimination. They argue that a decline of moral values among poor Blacks result in increased crime, illiteracy among Black youth, and higher incidences of single mother pregnancies. And, that callous indifference hurts development toward better, more complete, modern social conditions.

More importantly, they feel residing in the Black community would subject them to threatening and

139

uncontrollable life events. They also believe people like Jamaicans are backwards in terms of progress. Why? Many continue to express belief in (what White people call) pagan religions like voodoo. According to acculturating Blacks, Whites fail to consider poor Blacks as victims for those very reasons.

In contrast, they find less crime and violence important reasons for moving into affluent White communities. They also claim the larger society has an abundance of social support to reduce the effects of stress for acculturating minorities. And, such opportunities are good reasons to break loose from a neuroticism that binds them to dysfunctional behavior found in the Black community.

Yet, in the practice of longstanding Western tradition, racist perceptions dictate a need to limit adoption of Blacks into an established mainstream. It is worth noting, assimilation is a revoltingly gross expletive in the minds of many poor Black people. Dominant Whites are among the best educated in society yet highly ignorant of world cultures. Thus, they're the least civil-minded toward immigrant families, political refugees, and other minorities. In this regard, acculturating Blacks who move into historically White communities will continue to be affected by that perpetually thorny problem called racism.

Another characterization of poor Blacks is one describing them as wayward and unintelligible. Acculturating Blacks now occupy this mental attitude. Not surprisingly, they overlook the tragic fact that chronic living conditions set the contexts for how people consider Blacks. Inadequate housing, dangerous neighborhoods, burdensome responsibilities, and economic uncertainties contribute to America's unhealthy conceptions of poor Black people.

Often, but not inevitably, Blacks are victims in this way. On the one hand, genocide, suicide, and drug abuse shows the self-destructive nature of chronic living conditions. The situation of poverty can cause many to undergo confusion and anxiety. More often, the essential features of culture are lost and not replaced by those of the larger society. In this way, poor Black people are said to have no supportive base for effective coping. The loss of cultural meshing results in marginalization.

On the other hand, the problem and condition of discrimination, within a sociocultural context, sets the precedence for understanding their disrespectful mental attitude. In this case, discrimination means having to endure two unpleasant situations. First, poverty means having to depend on many overburdened and unresponsive bureaucratic systems. Such dependency contributes to a poor person's perception of powerlessness. Second, discrimination causes many poor Black people to reject the situation of poverty. They, in turn, feel the need to express concern for their stressful and unhealthy living conditions. Their response is often the desire to destroy America's social system and for its own sake. Religiosity, Black Nationalism, and extreme environmentalism, a more vulgar form of liberalism, are its results.

Those who practice extreme environmentalism consider environment to be a prime influence in the development of poor Black people. They make no qualms about the indurate attitude of poor Blacks, toward their own people, strangers, or others. In fact, extreme environmentalists make dutiful behavior appear less important than in actuality, according to conservatives.

I often refer to the disrespectful attitudes of poor Black people as cultural nihilism. A clear explanation for their mental reasoning is well in order. Nihilism occurs when people undergo confusion and anxiety for extended periods of time. Drug dealing, prostitution, and prison incarceration are more often its results. Genocide, suicide, and drug abuse are also common. Nihilists tend to overcompensate for their mental attitude by denying its impact rather than acknowledging the real reason for their failing situation.

In this case, *nihilism* is an affective component of denial that prevents people from experiencing painful thoughts. Simply, if you deny it, you won't have to feel bad about it: your situation or theirs. Most nearly, nihilism shows unreasonable and inordinate self-esteem or pride, a trait often shown when people are spurred on by societal members who dislike those said not to meet normative expectations on valued dimensions. In short, the thuggish mentality poor Black people adopt is, perhaps, an exaggerated effort to conceal a weakness.

In his award winning Grammy-hit, Ridin, Hakeem Seriki, better known by the stage name Chamillionaire, paints himself in a negative image considered by conservatives to be the norm for young Black males. He is assumed to be an American drug dealer carrying narcotics around the city in his flashy car. Said to have "no regard for the law," he is followed by police authorities. As the song progresses, a storyline unfolds. What Chamillionaire raps about in the song is a story of young Black males who are more often racially profiled by White police authority.

Many young Black males are usually pulled over for no apparent reason other than a DWB or **D**riving **W**hile **B**lack. Important to this plight is his ability to highlight problems of prejudice and discrimination often caused by White police abuse of authority. In fact, the need for today's Black youth to communicate their political views through the expression of music deeply shapes certain dimensions of their cultural identity. Curiously, while Chamillionaire calls to attention one problem of discrimination, the conservative class of acculturating Blacks reject the manner by which he chooses to convey it.

Acculturating Blacks claim messages, like the one rapper Chamillionaire communicates in his song, impacts how people consider Blacks as a whole. Further, they argue that the personal facade many Blacks present regards them as excessively adversarial. They believe that this mental impression, often presented by young Black males in today's society, more than justifies the actual practice of discrimination. But, they overlook the tragic fact White police abuse is a cultural response to the pervasive refusal of most Whites to treat Black people equal.

This major criticism is responsible not for a meaningful exchange of Black intellectual discourse, but conflict and new stressors between conservatives and liberals in Black leadership. In this way, conservatives close their minds to the mounting racial tensions and hostility reemerging between Whites and Blacks. That being said, if poor Blacks are considered by many to be backward in terms of Western progression, then the idea of conservatism becomes unacceptable.

Acculturating Blacks also argue that the refusal to understand their position does not allow them to be taken seriously by their own people. Ironically, they claim to be victims of Black adversity most nearly in the same way their poor Black adversaries claim White oppression. They claim to be discredited by liberals and poor Blacks who undermine sources of social support that play a key role in buffering the effects of severe stress for acculturating minorities.

Next, they say acculturating Blacks are made to endure personal attacks on their moral character. Why so? Many adopt conservative views. As a result, they feel their conservative efforts to educate and inform society about the plight and predicament of poor Blacks are greatly undermined by liberals and Blacks who more often refer to them as "Aunt Jemima and Uncle Tom" negro. This tragicomic situation in which they find themselves is said to prevent acculturating Blacks from lending their efforts to morally support poor Black people.

Certainly, liberals cannot be so indifferent to the suffering of others. The idea of community and wellness provide important opportunities for us to learn more about a situation that adversely affects the health of poor Black people and in so many different ways. Instead, liberals encourage acculturating Blacks to increase their effectiveness in working with poor Blacks, to build stronger relationships with them, identify their needs, and dedicate resources to programs that specifically benefit members of the community.

Community and wellness programs function, effectively, to improve the health of poor Blacks, enabling them to cope with stress. Liberals believe when we empower the poor through community resources, like health and wellness programs, it creates a supportive base for the severe stress of poverty and discrimination. Unfortunately, when conservative or acculturating Blacks withdraw themselves from the Black community, they indirectly sabotage activities meant to bring about progressive change.

Conservative class, acculturating Blacks slow down the progressive efforts of those seeking to control potent stressors in the lives of poor Black people. For instance, they are unlikely to support the President on initiatives that work to improve wellness in the Black community. They're also reluctant to become involved in healthcare programs that require long-term financial cost. More importantly, their closed-minded views reinforce support for structural barriers that deny poor Black people rights to access.

Therefore, acculturating Blacks fail to show concern for the stress of poverty and discrimination, an inconsideration that adversely affects health and wellness among poor Black people. The problem with relations between acculturating and poor Blacks may then be conservative ideals reinforce strong dislike for community and wellness. In this way, poor Blacks may show no interest in or concern for conservatives or Post Party Conservatism cautious that the movement may work a subtle poison in its usually injurious way.

As a result, many believe embodying conservative ideals will put the Black community at a danger of loss, harm, or failure. Only when the conservative class of acculturating Blacks increase their effectiveness in working with poor Blacks, can we consider their ideals vitally important mechanisms to resolving health and wellness problems in the Black community. But, how can we help foster positive messages within minority communities?

I believe it was Robert E. Slavin, sometime in the new millennium, who best said (and I'm paraphrasing) what we need is to ensure community members are on equal footing so as to create peaceful expressions of resolutions. It is the responsibility of the community to reduce conflict so it can grow, instill community reliance, establish self-help programs, and bring new resolutions to historical problems.

Poor coping mechanisms can only bring more violence to already disadvantaged neighborhoods. Peer groups and self-help programs will establish some form of relationship where communities can, in fact, participate. Slavin goes on to say that today's communities recognize the need for change. And, in some way, most have constructed intergroup relations to resolve problems aimed at restoring community pride and integrity.

The Race Relations Forum was created in Cleveland Ohio by community leaders from forty neighborhoods to help people address racial prejudice and discrimination. Public and intergroup relations training were conducted for local businesses, clergy, and police authorities in local districts. The Anti-defamation league of New Haven, Connecticut created *A World of Difference* program, which addresses many community issues head-on.

Finally, Slavin purports the direction a community faces is, in reality, up to its local residents. Civil health and positive intergroup relations are usually the end result of cooperative learning and respect for cultural diversity. When equal footing can be established, both businesses and community residents greatly benefit.

Chapter 5
Several Key Issues Affecting Blacks and their
Support for Homosexual Rights

As a gay male, my sexual orientation also marginalized me and made me feel like an outcast, made me feel less than human. ... The gay community worldwide has a history, although it is constantly being attacked and ignored. But, sadly, lesbian, gay, bisexual, transgender, and queer Italian Americans do not have a history... a recorded history that is. Yes, we exist, but our existence has not been recorded, read, and studied, thoroughly, with sincerity and respect. ... Do gay Italian Americans disgrace their families? The answer is yes and no; thus, a paradox is formed.

Michael Carosone (2012)

In the psychology textbook *The Fundamentals of Abnormal Psychology*, written by Ronald J. Comer (1996), he says the gay community exists in various dimensions of culture. There is nothing new about gay people or their lifestyles. Unfortunately, the way in which they live continues to spark controversy. Most people do not openly support gay lifestyles. Yet, few people condemned it throughout history. Why is there still controversy surrounding the growing acceptance of gay lifestyles? The state of being gay or *homosexuality* is a physical attraction to people of one's own sex.

In this thesis, we will engage in a lively controversy on several key issues affecting Blacks and their support for homosexual rights. A special note of importance: Gay is now the standard term for homosexual and is preferred by homosexual men. As a result, it is now very difficult to use the term "gay" in its earlier meanings (carefree or bright and showy) without arousing a sense of double entendre. Gay, in its modern sense, typically refers to men; lesbian is the standard term used for homosexual women.

151

One of several key issues affecting support for homosexual rights is the debate over whether they choose to engage in relationships with members of their own sex or does biology factor into their lifestyle. This debate is fueled by many people to include researchers from the scientific community. Comer purported that in 1973, homosexuality was listed in the Diagnostic and Statistic Manual for Mental Disorders (DSM) as a sexual disorder. Homosexual rights coalition groups and psychotherapists protested against it. The American Psychological Association (APA) eventually dismissed homosexuality as a sexual disorder. However, newer editions of the DSM did retain a category called ego dystonic homosexuality. The category was dropped most recently. Today, psychotherapists largely accept homosexuality as a variant of normal sexual behavior, not a sexual disorder.

Comer further says the gay community believes they should be accorded the same rights as heterosexuals since sexual orientation is the only notable variable that differentiates their behavior from what is considered ordinary. They even made demands for access to housing reserved for couples-only and for spouse coverage in health insurance, which are being upheld in courts. Henceforth, the gay community has fought what appears to be a winning battle for their equal rights. These issues are important to gay couples in the same way they affect heterosexual couples.

Comer reminds us that in the 1990's, "outing" the private lives and affairs of famous people took place. As the government sought to reduce prejudice and racism, many issues regarding the acceptance of homosexuals were going unnoticed. *Gay bashing*, a term used to describe homosexual men who were beaten and killed even, failed to catch media attention. Drastic measures called for homosexual rights activists to "out" public figures whose sexual orientation were unknown at the time. Outing eventually led President Bill Clinton to repeal the military's policy regarding homosexuality. Despite a winning victory for the gay community, there is continued controversy surrounding their growing acceptance.

It appears America continues to discriminate against homosexuals. Yet, they continue to survive and flourish. They continue to show remarkable resilience and adaptation in the face of overwhelming adversity. Certainly, we are not saying hatred of homosexuals no longer exists. In stark contrast, hate crimes are on the rise. They will continue to occur with the prevailing trend in social climate. As a result, it has become more acceptable for people to express opened hatred for lesbians and gays.

The information network highway now serves as a recruiting aid in discriminating against anyone considered less than acceptable. The Internet also serves as a method of teaching, exchanging information, and developing contacts for people who, due to social pressure, would not otherwise express their discriminatory views.

Computer bulletin boards offer tips on anti-gay strategies to prevent homosexuals from establishing civil rights. With the help of encrypted codes, new members can also acquire tips on how to militarize personal tactics on gay rights prevention. And, through election campaigns, contemporary themes of isolationism, nationalism, and ultraconservative Christian fundamentalism serves as simple means of opportunities in which hate groups can begin to reestablish, reaffect, and reaffirm indirect participation in discordant, less than productive relations with mainstream culture. Such strategies are especially true in terms of gender identity and public policy.

Hate crimes, criminal actions we link to race, ethnicity, culture, and other ascribed identities are intended to threaten the core of a community. For instance, Matthew Wayne Shepard, a student from the University of Wyoming, was beaten and murdered in Laramie (1998) for being openly gay. Shepard's murder brought national and international attention to hate crimes. It compelled President Barack Obama to sign legislation for the Matthew Shepard and James Byrd, Jr. Hate Crimes Act, which passed into law on October 28, 2009.

Each hate crime affects how homosexuals and other minorities respond in the larger society. Hate crimes differ from other criminal offenses in that the offender, whether intentionally or unintentionally, sends a disturbing message to members of the target group. Since hate groups would like to free the United States and all European territory of nonwhites and those considered less acceptable, the action sends a message to those who are perceived to oppose core White values, like Blacks, Jews, Asians, and homosexuals.

In fact, what is significant about the intent of hate crimes is an unfortunate group is now unwelcome and unsafe in a particular environment. Hate crimes hurt specific individuals and members of the group simultaneously. In this way, people who are targeted because of inherent differences can be made to feel powerless. As well, they can experience distrust.

Homosexuals can develop stress and oppression. The suffering can involve intergroup or psychological conflict. In this case, group relations will destabilize, requiring a resolution. First, social maladjustment may occur, resulting in emotional instability. Homicide, suicide, family abuse, and substance abuse can occur. The kind of maladjustment reached appears to weigh heavily on how homosexuals cope in the larger society. However, such influences do not mean all homosexuals will have problems coping in the face of stress and oppression. Rather, they may come to ignore the rich diversity and complexity of smaller cultural groups.

In response, a few homosexuals will conform in accordance with the traditional values upheld by their oppressors. Why so? They believe it will help them better cope and survive in the larger society. They may even completely lose their sense of self in their efforts to cope and adapt.

How might homosexuals cope to prevent themselves from losing their sense of self? Why does controversy continue to surround homosexuals despite their growing acceptance? Why have a significant portion of minorities failed to consider homosexual rights? What issues do people have with supporting the gay community? Perhaps, how they cope in the face of adversity can give us special insight. The rest of this chapter should shed light on several key issues affecting Blacks and their support for homosexual rights.

An important depiction of Black American families living in inner city environments reveal a few important survival strategies used to cope and adapt. They have shown remarkable resilience and adaptation by developing their own communities and social structures. Kin systems, churches, and family associations are often developed to help buffer the stress in their lives. In addition, Blacks highly value the family as a mutual support system. They also help to improve social awareness, adhere to the American work ethic, and view religion as a source of strength.

The Black church is largely used as a way of coping with stress. As an institution, it has a long history in Black culture, with roots in the slave experience. The Black church became a substitution for fulfilling certain needs and functions once satisfied by village-based religion and social structures, community-oriented activities Black people brought over with them from Africa. The Black church has become a staple in their efforts to cope with stress, especially valuing religion above all else.

In contrast, the supportive base necessary for effective coping is removed from homosexuals once they reveal their gender identity. In this way, they have become an acceptable means of expressing hatred. Thus, whenever homosexuals develop ways of coping, their efforts are met with resistance, and from people we'd least expect.

African Americans were greatly criticized in debate by Libertarians (2012). In 2008 Blacks took, what many people in the United States called, a conservative stance on one of the most important issues to emerge since the Supreme Court ruling against segregation (1967). Their decision, as some liberals believe, is remarkably close to the principles of segregationist Whites like Bull Connor.

However, there were several key issues affecting their support for homosexual rights. Hence, the perception of Blacks as conservative, resistant, even hostile to government propositions that could ultimately improve the quality of living for a people, is a gross misconception. Conservatism lends itself to those who foster anti-gay attitudes and propagate myths about their lifestyles. Still, there is something misguided about Black Americans and their conceptions of homosexuals.

Today, African Americans continue to have difficulty achieving equality. And, de facto segregation continues to exist. Yet, they refuse to show support for homosexual rights. Liberals feel African Americans should understand better than any combination of competing groups, the need to support homosexual rights. After all, they continue to suffer greatly from the adverse effects of severe stress and oppression.

Liberals believe that Black people were being hypocrites by arguing the importance of minority rights while at the same time dismissing homosexual rights. They felt such beliefs and opinions were groundless and unacceptable with any common sense reasoning. In addition, liberals argue homosexual rights should be awarded by reason of citizenship. Same-sex marriage, as a civil rights issue, is a civil union and protected under the United States constitution. Same-sex marriage was upheld by the Supreme Court in June of 2015.

Liberals, undoubtedly, believe Black Americans should be accepting of homosexual rights. Liberals believe Blacks should be more than understanding. Why? They continue to have difficulty reaching equality more than any cultural group on earth. Specifically, when gay bashing led to the murder of more than seventy-three lesbians and gays just because they were gender different, Blacks should immediately sympathize with the nature of their tragedy.

Paradoxically, that implication suggests homo-sexuals and Blacks have undergone the same adversities. Still, how can African Americans resist supporting a progressive movement like homosexual rights or civil unions? Nevertheless, the vast majority of Blacks argue, vehemently, against homosexual rights, contributing gay lifestyles to an expected and inessential problem of Whites.

As for conservatives, they view homosexual rights as problematic. In this way, they inadvertently contribute to a greater problem. Conservatives talk about homosexual rights as if it were a matter for only a select group of individuals. They fail to consider the aggregate of lesbian, gay, bisexual, and transgender (LGBT) people who form their own communities, towns, and cities.

As LGBT groups took root in small areas, they simply passed on their knowledge and values to each other. The knowledge and values, which originally taught homosexuals how to behave, think, and feel, became their culture. As a result, they built, shaped, and carved out their own communities. In creating their own spaces, homosexual lifestyles progressed from the socially rejected to a low and steady rise of acceptance.

Today, the gay community continues to help form a new society. They cope and adapt to life in America even though conservatives exercise their power to exclude them from civil liberties. LGBT groups are cooperating within a larger social system in their efforts to move into the established mainstream. Tomorrow, they might just become mainstream.

For homosexuals to show remarkable courage in the face of overwhelming adversity serves as a source of inspiration for some people. Some people feel homosexuals are a kind of model for those who feel their cultural identity is lost. Homosexuals have shown they are capable of changing their environment to fit their own needs. However, liberals feel the "gay movement" cannot serve as significant historical and social importance while people in society continue to disregard LGBT group issues, especially those who are extremely influential.

Conservatives view LGBT groups as cultural minorities. This experience includes a narrowing of life's opportunities that go far beyond any shortcoming homosexuals may possess. They have no share, aside from their cultural beliefs and opinions, in what the larger society considers valuable. They are defined by unequal treatment, distinguished gender traits, involuntary membership, awareness of inferiority, and lack of rights. Here, to acknowledge the gay community is taboo.

In the military, instead of recognizing lesbians and gays, they created *"Don't Ask, Don't Tell"* policies. Such policies prevented many people from openly serving in the Armed Forces. Thanks to homosexual rights, campaigning, and the efforts of President Obama, *"Don't Ask, Don't Tell"* was repealed. Today, lesbian and gay military personnel now serve their country, openly, without having to hide their gender identity. While it is true we have come a long way with regard to homosexual rights, many Black Americans continue to show resistance on key issues affecting support for homosexual rights. To gain a better understanding for why White logic is at variance with Black reasoning, consider the below overview.

This overview highlights several key issues affecting support for homosexual rights in the Black community. That many Black people are unsupportive of LGBT groups is critical to understanding how we might overcome any adversities against homosexuality. We also need to gain a better understanding of Black communities and social structures, network support systems that might impact their perspectives despite the growing acceptance of homosexuals. Further, we need to emphasize the Black church as a source of strength as well as take into consideration the impact of stress and oppression.

Each progression factors into the human psyche, which can explain why many Black Americans choose not to support LGBT groups in their fight for equal rights. Similarly, it appears more conservatives do not understand the need to support homosexuals in their fight for equal rights. In fact, a major problem for LGBT groups in the United States is resistance to change often imposed by fearful conservatives.

Also, despite political differences that exist between LGBT groups and Black Americans, both are labeled minority by the larger dominant society. To understand key issues affecting support for homosexual rights in the Black community, the following problems need to be taken into account:

- Black people face considerable adversity as they continue to cope and survive life in the larger dominant society.

- As a marker of poverty, they are continuously discriminated against by the larger dominant society, even among cultural groups to include homosexuals.

- The church is their strongest source of strength so they value it above all else.

The United States has too often been a burial ground for aspiring people. People move to North America in hopes of becoming an integral part of the larger culture. Such efforts reveal information on how LGBT groups might cope and adapt to life in America. Perhaps the most important of key issues affecting Blacks and their support for homosexual rights is religion. However, their position is ostensibly biblical in nature. That is, on the surface, it may appear to be religious reasoning that prevents them from supporting homosexual rights. But underneath, religious reasoning is not necessarily the case.

Many Blacks believe the reason not to support homosexual rights is sustained by the very doctrines of Christian religion. An institution that teaches love, peace, and tranquility, the church has since been a fortress against homosexuals and their rights to civil liberties. The church was introduced to Black Americans through the religious teachings of Protestant Whites who followed Judeo-Christianity. Perhaps the most fundamental principle of Christianity teaches us marriage is the religious union between a man and a woman.

Today, the church has ingrained its fundamental principles into the very fabric of Black reasoning. Therefore, Blacks may not be willing to abandon, perhaps, the most sacred principle of the church. In fact, church goers often believe gay rights are marked by immorality and perversion.

Another key issue to emerge in debate as a possible explanation is Blacks may have mixed feelings or emotions about supporting homosexual rights. Black Americans may have a general ambivalence about supporting any practice condemned by the church. While a few church going Blacks openly endorse homosexual rights, many believe supporting it has costly implications.

The church considers the practice an abomination. In this way, it is more likely Blacks may sympathize with problems most homosexuals face but also feel God will persecute anyone who supports an unaccepted practice. Further, they may feel LGBT groups contribute to their own problems by choosing to embrace homosexuality. What's so sad about church goers is their failure to understand people are not homosexual by choice.

Another key issue affecting support for homosexual rights among Black Americans is the debate over whether LGBT groups are genuine about supporting minority rights. Skepticism exists across cultural groups. A great many Black Americans in the coming generation will not endorse homosexual rights unless there are compromises and concessions made to reduce racial tension.

Racial tension continues to spark conflict and hatred among Blacks, Whites, strangers, and others. For Black people, the lack of support is more about acquiring that which is deserved or due. They have longingly awaited Whites to reconsider the moral obligations of a society in which minority rights are ignored. They argue the attitude of Blacks pushing too hard and too fast for equality, making unfair demands for change, and getting undeserved special attention from government agencies that support minority rights to public office and access to public accommodations, like fair housing and so forth, are unjust.

They question, how can a society that calls its members just continue to ignore minority rights and yet consider a practice long since condemned by their own religion? They believe redefining homosexual rights to suit the desires and needs of LGBT groups is unprincipled. In addition, many believe that to equate Black morality with homosexuality demeans the efforts of all who supported the civil rights movement. It also implies Black people have morally objectionable behavior, not worthy of consideration. In this way, Black Americans, in their own attempts to eliminate inequality, continue their struggle, and without the aid of LGBT groups. In brief, many Black Americans continue to take what appears to be a conservative stance against homosexual rights on the moral grounds of equality or fairness.

Still, another key issue affecting support for homosexual rights require yet a closer inspection of Black people. In this way, we can build on a praiseworthy concept, one that has yet to be verified, but if proven, would be morally obligatory. Allow me to explain.

Americans need to understand marginalization imposes considerable stress on Black people. Chronic living conditions are strong stressors in their lives. These conditions: infant mortality, incarceration, teenage pregnancy, and violent crime, for instance, may contribute to their perception of powerlessness.

In addition, they may experience considerable confusion and anxiety. Why? The essential features of their identity are lost and not replaced by those of the larger society. Many Blacks have lost cultural and psychological contact with both their traditional society and the larger dominant society. In response, they have become marginal. The stress caused by not being assimilated or integrated into an established mainstream more often leaves them feeling alienated and with a loss of identity.

Today, marginalization includes loss of fulfillment once met by religious-based practices and community organizations. These feelings become more stressful. Stress occurs as a result of having no selective involvement from either cultural system, systems that can provide Black people with the supportive base for effective coping. Although social networks offer some protection in certain situations, it may be especially stressful for those in conflict.

Unfortunately, the support of communities and social structures may not be enough to improve their adaptive responses. Marginalization is an indication that chronic living conditions more likely contributes to Black people having unsupportive attitudes toward acculturating groups—for instance, homosexuals and their movement to become an integral part of the larger society. It is a major problem that exists for Blacks, but in the contexts of White hypocrisy.

Who was willing to support homosexuals and the LGBT rights movement? Where did President Obama stand on the issue of homosexual rights? Did he support the gay community or not? Past Presidents refused to cooperate with or endorse LGBT groups on the issue of homosexual rights. Society continues to view homosexuals as having extremely unimportant experiences for the existence of America.

Today, homosexuals face considerable stress from rejection in their lives. Yet, in the face of stress and rejection, they too show remarkable adaptiveness, resilience, responsibility, and coping skills. Not so far in the past, LGBT pride prevented homosexual persons from accepting endorsements from heterosexuals? Most people, not just those who seek social awareness and cultural literacy, can stand to benefit from a more accurate understanding.

LGBT groups lobbied for equal rights in the United States well into the new millennium. Yet, they rejected important endorsements. Coretta Scott King, the widow of Dr. Martin Luther King Jr., DD, called gay marriage a civil rights issue as she denounced a proposed constitutional amendment that would ban it. Unfortunately, after learning of Mrs. King's endorsement for LGBT rights, White supporters from both homosexual and heterosexual communities placed distance between themselves and the civil rights movement by calling their movement a "human rights agenda."

Now ask yourself, for the more than eight thousand African Americans murdered in the name of equal rights, how can White people not support Blacks and their effort to eliminate racial inequality? Never mind the gay community discriminates against every cultural group in America to gain acceptance. Also, they continue to show resistance toward social programs that would help protect minority rights.

For instance, Affirmative Action and school desegregation are two social programs that can help minorities reach full equality. In contrast, perhaps their prejudice is not so much an insult to Black Americans, many of whom cannot claim to have dealt very effectively or fairly with understanding homosexuals and their position.

Due to the way Black people resist homosexuality, Libertarians try to undermine the most important question confronting Blacks today: Will they ever support a practice condemned by the church, a decision some people feel threatens to further disadvantage them, reduce their social status, and deny greater opportunities or equal rights?

As Blacks continue to develop impressive strategies for coping with living in America, they continue to struggle with their position on homosexual rights. They believe the issue of homosexual rights is undertaken without regard to how it affects human dignity and decency. Most significantly, President Obama tried to end any chance of continued debate taking place.

On May 10, 2012, President Obama gave his endorsement for the Civil Marriage Protection Act. His support for LGBT rights depended, largely, on fundamental changes in the church and American lifestyles. To put it bluntly, his decision rested on a cultural revival of free will for the gay community. Yet, while Blacks work to have greater material comfort and political freedom, requisites for meaningful Black progress, LGBT groups would have the power to make free choices unconstrained by government and religious bureaucracies. To spite this progression, supporters of traditional marriage prepared for a 2012 referendum.

Supporters of traditional marriage did not wait on state agencies to act with regard to the President's endorsement for homosexual rights. Instead, they requested the petitioned signatures of registered voters for a referendum. The referendum was a direct popular vote used to stop government agencies, like the Maryland House of Delegates, from approving a bill that would legalize same-sex marriages in the church. In places like Maryland, supporters of traditional marriage collected more than fifty thousand petitioned signatures. Despite strong resistance from critics, The Civil Rights Protection Act passed on Tuesday, November 6, 2012.

President Obama tried to put an end to this lively controversy for these two reasons: First, if ever there was in existence a taboo found among Blacks it is LGBT rights, a topic most refuse to talk about openly and honestly. This failure obscures the positive role of LGBT groups. Why so? It often reflects conservative ideals in the narrow-minded way White Americans discuss race. We are not born with an identity. Our identities are ascribed to us through socialization. Therefore, one of the most important responsibilities a culture can have is to assist its members in forming their own identities. What a culture seeks to preserve and pass on to the next generation can tell us much about its moral character.

The second reason President Obama stepped in and intervened on LGBT rights was constitutional. Equality is a right or rights belonging to all people by reason of citizenship, especially the fundamental freedoms and privileges guaranteed by the 13th, 14th, and 15th amendments. Perhaps Black Americans, in their focus on the church and self-preservation, show no understanding of constitutional law. Why? They adhere to self-serving principles according to which they are motivated by self-interest as the foundation of morality.

The church has a system of values and moral principles by which we all tend to live. It is instrumental in increasing self-esteem, raising awareness about one's self-importance, and creating a strong sense of identity. It is through the interpretation of church that Blacks, an oppressed people extremely desirous for recognition, choose to establish their cultural identity, achieve greater liberty, and confront inequality. Unfortunately, religious devotion by church going Black folk enables them to ignore LGBT rights as if homosexuals do not love God or make religious sacrifices. Or, perhaps, Blacks simply understand that the establishment of LGBT rights and the message it carries falls under family, community, and church. Each way decides how our values are preserved. In many minds, the comparison between gay sacrifice and Black suffrage is unfair.

Many Black Americans believe it is wrong to equate homosexuality with Black morality. They assert it is an incredible disregard for their everyday circumstances, especially against Blacks who are greatly disadvantaged. Pay attention and take careful notice that the oppression of slavery and the system of segregation are unique to African Americans. The eugenics movement and American racism are also part of the Black experience.

Today, Whites continue to show hostility and hatred toward Black people due to their skin color. Homosexuals, on the other hand, are discriminated against. Why? Their love and sacrifice conflict with Western traditions. Thus, they simply lost their place among dominant Whites in the hierarchy of traditional values.

To juxtapose contrasting arguments, many Blacks feel deprived. Why? America called for LGBT rights while Black people have yet to reach full equality. Many more feel wronged. Why? They continue to cope and survive at the minimum level of subsistence below which people should not be expected to exist. In this way, their everyday circumstances do not explain why a group that is most vocal and best organized against discrimination has not won greater political and economic freedom. Still, there are those in the coming generation who feel that, in comparison to others, Blacks have yet to benefit from the rights of free will.

Sadly, Blacks are not getting their fair share in life. This form of inequality is a matter of resistance. For them, the establishment of LGBT rights means White people now accept homosexuals, but not yet Blacks living in America. Since the President would consider granting economic wellness and political freedom to lesbians, gays, bisexuals, and transgender individuals without protecting the civil liberties of Blacks who continue to suffer (i.e., as they continue to cope and adapt to life in America) under conditions of absolute deprivation and political powerlessness, is absurd.

Until we learn to celebrate the richness of diversity and to appreciate sharing our values with people who differ, it is not possible to develop a better understanding of ourselves. A few Black Americans feel that if homosexuals would like more people to support their "agenda" in the future, perhaps they should take care not to discriminate against Blacks, a racial group that can effect positive change for a people facing overwhelming adversity.

In the case of discrimination, Black people can certainly show homosexuals, those having supposed unnatural identities, how to cope and adapt to life. Remember, it was conservative Whites, law-biding and God-fearing Christians, who made the most damning arguments against LGBT rights. Condemning arguments were also made when Former President George W. Bush, Jr. proposed a constitutional amendment that would forever place a ban on same-sex marriage in America. As for Blacks and their issues affecting support for LGBT rights, opposing arguments continue to exist in a love and hate relationship between church and state.

How can we close cultural gaps that exist among homosexuals, Blacks, and the rest of society? We can start by bettering our relationships with one another. Through interaction, we can improve our communication skills, increase social awareness, understand certain attitudes and beliefs as well as support minority rights to important accommodations, like fair housing, and so forth. We can also be more accepting of each other in our efforts to reach a greater equality of opportunity. Although our cultural beliefs and opinions may appear absurd on the surface, prejudice, discrimination, and victimization have a tremendous impact on how we cope in the face of overwhelming adversity.

Many explanations were given during the debate on several key issues affecting Blacks and their support for homosexual rights. America's discomfort, uneasiness, and fear of change greatly contributes to why many Americans fail to show their support. However, people should be assimilated or integrated into Western society rather than ignored at the risk of marginalization.

Chapter 6
In the Age of Trumpism: A Backlash of Hostility

And when you're a star, they let you do it. You can do anything. I just grab'em by the pussy.

Donald J. Trump
In Conversation with then
Access Hollywood Host
Billy Bush (2005)

Three years after the Obama Administration and Democrats were still in awe. They continued to experience cognitive dissonance over the new President and his Administration. Dissonance was triggered by a nation built on the idea of equality yet, in some way, feared change. His election contradicted the popular vote; and, it occurred without explanation from the Electoral College.

To exacerbate matters, America appeared to be in great conflict. Fighting over the building of a border-wall, the nuclear disarmament of Kim Jong Un's communist North Korea, a daunting task, and greater disparity along identity lines tore at the very fabric of American democracy.

Republicans continued to undermine any attempt to awaken America to its ugly xenophobic resentment. Efforts to undo their unyielding, pitiless resistance often came under attack. Why? It was due to the continued inappropriateness of Republican lawmakers who relied on confirmation bias rather than hard facts. The lack of openness to evaluation by Democrats led to a gross falsification of American politics.

Curiously, it was conservatives in the Republican Party who continued to make excuses for America's vicious past. The result was Donald J. Trump, a living testimony to the fact that America continued to breed a culture of denial.

Trump successfully appealed his proposition to an untapped audience of frustrated voters. Many appeared to be divided along racial, ethnic, cultural, and national identity lines. The Republican strategy was to rely on confirmation bias. Trump relied on rigorous attempts at refutation to elicit voters. His campaign consisted of statements, beliefs, and claims said to be both factual and necessary. He often characterized his opponents' claims as contradictory, exaggerated or, sometimes, seemingly unfalsifiable, but also extremely unlikely to ever be confirmed.

Many Trump supporters voted, perhaps, for the first time in decades. Others would vote on a Republican candidate for the first time, ever. It was Trump and his seemingly genuine concern for their personal wellness that attracted voters, experts said. Along with his openness and willingness to restore a nation to greatness, Trump attracted generations of voters otherwise unexploited.

American families experienced mental discomfort over the current state of affairs, which contradicted their belief system. Talk of catastrophic school shootings by nihilists made many suffer discomfort. Murders carried out by gang members left more feeling uneasy about their living conditions. For others, the housing market collapse of 2008 left them in fear and in their own homes.

Trump needed to motivate his audience effectively and persuasively. His answer for solving their problems was to build a border-wall. In this way, he could convince generations that a wall on the US Mexico border was necessary. In fact, Trump comforted American families for first time since the era of President Ronald W. Reagan.

Many believed a wall was the answer to keeping out undocumented immigrants, lawless criminals, and drug gang members. But, he was constantly accused of being bigoted for taking such controversial actions. Although he always denied any form of bigotry, it would be Trump's continuous involvement in scandals and cover-ups that received widespread exposure.

Accusations of sexual misconduct surfaced during the Trump campaign. Trump's alleged attitude toward women was inexcusable. The most egregious accusations of sexual misconduct were from women he met in the 1980's. Sexual assault, sexual harassment, and groping were among the many accusations alleged over the years. At least nineteen women made accusations against Trump.

He has since denied any and all accusations. Trump insisted that he was the victim of media bias, conspiracies, and a political smear campaign. The first woman to accuse Trump of sexual misconduct during his presidential campaign was Alva Johnson.

Multiple women came forth with accusations of sexual misconduct. Since the 2005 sexual assault charge was made against Trump—a claim in which case he gave his accounts of kissing and groping women against their will—more women came forward to publically accuse the Republican nominee of sexual misconduct.

By his own admission, Trump mentioned he never waited for permission to kiss or touch women, saying "I don't even wait... I just grab 'em by the pussy!" Subsequently, he characterized his comments as "locker room talk."

Afterward, Trump denied having any such encounters with women. He also apologized for making lewd comments toward them. Many women stated that Trump's denial made them come forth with more accusations of sexual misconduct.

More accusations appeared during his presidential campaign. This time, accusations of inappropriate behavior surfaced from two beauty pageant contestants. Miss USA and Miss Teen USA contestants both said Trump entered their dressing rooms at which time they would be at various stages of undress.

Donald Trump, who owned the Miss Universe franchise, which hosted both pageants, was accused of inappropriate behavior from the years 1997 to 2006. In a 2005 interview with Howard Stern, Trump claimed he had enough influence to get away with inappropriate behavior.

Usually, accusations would have enough impact on the credibility of a presidential candidate. But, conservatives were quick to say no arguments could be drawn from the appropriateness or inappropriateness of Trump's behavior. Why?

His accusations differed from people who were illicit in that his inappropriateness did not necessarily have any accompanying legal ramifications. In this way, meager accusations of misconduct were not enough to force the candidate out of a US presidential race. But, that's not to say Americans weren't scandalized when they were made aware of his blatant breaches of moral norms and business practices.

Members of both political parties were insulted as many felt the candidate lacked a certain quality of suitability befitting a US President. They understood that with Donald Trump in office, their struggles would meet only the unbending, pitiless resistance of conservatism.

To the contrary, talk of an unfit President was met by angry denials from unsuspecting supporters. Trump's campaign managers were heavily criticized for denying the serious nature of the accusations. Scandals broke out in many states over voting rights. But, the hardest part was Trump's border-wall proposal, which denied rights of access to undocumented immigrant children.

Still, the presidential candidate refused to withdraw from the presidential race. Instead, he issued a flat denial of any and all accusations made against him. And, with the support of conservatives, Trump put forth a plausible campaign.

His campaign slogan, Make America Great Again, helped Trump rally enough support around American families suffering from a worsening economy. He swore to restore that which was established, to preserve what was traditional, and to limit change. He also promised to preserve the heritage of a once great nation.

Despite the duration of protest, Trump received strong reactions, with some people praising him as a man best worthy of serving America's interest while others highlighting the continualness of his inappropriate behavior. Luckily, the uncompromising demands of partisan politics would work in his favor as many families developed a biased, emotional allegiance to him.

Although he was slighted by members of both political parties, conservative partisan members were not swayed enough to redirect their vote. On November 8, 2016, the Electoral College elected Donald J. Trump into the Oval Office as America's 45th President.

Before entering the US presidential race (2016), Donald John Trump was a successful businessman and television personality. However, his observations were often followed by inexperience in which case he drew inappropriate attention to himself by making vulgar remarks about minorities. His nasty comments, combined with proud, self-serving remarks, more often led him to legitimize discrimination. Trump became widely viewed as someone who exacerbated racial anxieties in the United States.

On the campaign trail is where Trump developed a reputation for insulting women, minorities, and people with disabilities. Of the many controversies, people felt Trump's lowest moment took place when he mocked the disabled news reporter, Serge Kovaleski, a person living with arthrogryposis, a hereditary trait affecting the joints.

Democrats were quick to counter Trump's inappropriateness by extolling the virtues of the Democratic Party. They informed the public that humanity requires we treat the disabled not as burdens, but work together to develop better public policy. In working together, we continuously build better opportunities for them and a stronger united front for everyone. In this way, some experts believed we would have a greater chance to instigate social change.

Trump and his self-styled pirate approach to politics ignited a backlash of hostility. His style had a profound impact on the thinking strategy of dominant White America. Conservatives were most impressed with the way he stage-managed his entire campaign. White identity politics were staged to look like it came from a culture of victimization.

Conservatives were said to be victims of hoaxes, trigger warnings, and trauma-informed communities that sprang up in defense of dishonest people. Many Trump supporters believed that Republicans created conservatism as the endgame to America's social problems. The result was any demands made for equality would be manipulated into a suffering backlash of White-victimization.

Conservatives were quick to respond as victims against movements like Black Lives Matter (#BLM). Catchphrases like All Lives Matters and Blue Lives Matters appeared as the two most well-known rhetorical expressions of the backlash. Both catchphrases undermined

Black people's attempts to influence public policy in favor of change.

The backlash was a major disruption in the attempt to destabilize any movement seeking to influence public policy. Media coverage and political responses seemingly worked to fuel the backlash of angry voters. And, while White America claimed to be a culture of victimization, their cries were merely antagonistic reactions to progressive movements concerned with instigating social change.

Trump exploited the backlash. He did so, and from what many critics thought was a small audience of frustrated voters. Many voters were quick to defend his reputation. They genuinely believed the backlash developed from Whites having to endure a culture of victimization.

In stark contrast, it was formed as an antagonistic reaction to angry feelings found among conservatives within the Republican Party. The problem was many conservatives were angry at having to defend White privilege. White privilege had been front and center during the civil rights movement as was true for Black Lives Matter.

Curiously, Black Lives Matter was organized in the face of criticism. It originated in the Black community as an activist movement. As an international movement, Black Lives Matter proved to be a greater success than many critics anticipated. Its mission was to campaign against the backlash of violence and systemic racism, which aimed to oppress Black people.

The catchphrase or hash tag All Lives Matter sprang up as an antagonistic reaction to the Black Lives Matter movement. On the surface, it served as a declaration of independence from historical racism. It also appeared to welcome as an institution of civil thought, better attitudes toward racial equality and social justice.

While on the campaign trail in Missouri, Presidential nominee Hillary R. Clinton faced a backlash of criticism after she used the phrase at a historically Black church. She was heavily criticized for dismissing or belittling the message that Black Lives Matter.

All Lives Matter was supposed to be a testimony of colorblindness. Colorblind societies were not supposed to view skin color in different racial groups a deficit. It was thought to be based on a new political ideology that openly condemned historical racism. This new school of thought was said to reject discrimination with every intention to discredit racism, prejudice, homophobia, et cetera.

But upon closer inspection, it represented America's refusal to acknowledge an unpleasant reality, that is to say, all lives did not matter. When Whites changed Black Lives Matter to All Lives Matter, it demonstrated a failure to understand the system of structural racism. The implication was all lives were equally at risk. Yet, all lives were not, a demeaning message that trivialized suffering among Blacks as defeatist and tacit.

Black people continued to be confronted by structural barriers that denied their rights to access. They were often denied access to quality housing, healthcare, employment, and education just to name a few potent stressors in their lives.

Racial disparities also pervaded the legal system in America, undermining its relevance as a delivery of justice. To adamantly understand structural racism is to know Black lives are devalued in America. Conservatives show their inappropriateness when they attempt to remove race from the equation.

Yet, Black Lives Matter was criticized by prominent figures like Bill O'Relly, Rudy Giuliani, and then Presidential candidate Donald Trump. They felt the movement was disruptive and conflict-ridden. That it was designed with the intention to cause disagreement that separated Americans into opposing groups.

Donald Trump purported that Black Lives Matter was a racially divisive term. During his campaign, Trump tweeted misinformation that apparently showed Black people accounted for more than 95 percent of the murders in Black communities and about 80 percent of the murders that took place in White communities. In contrast, his information contradicted statistical evidence found by the Federal Bureau Investigation (FBI) and its Uniform Crime Report.

Bill O'Relly said that Black Lives Matter was a destructive movement. He felt that the movement was one capable of producing violent emotions, arousing controversies, and inciting strong reactions. He claimed its leaders were people who viewed America as an inherently evil country based on White supremacy. He further believed the leadership did not want to resolve social conflicts but wanted to destroy its existence. The problem with Black Lives Matter, then, was its inability to unite Americans along identity lines.

Former Mayor Rudolph W. Giuliani charged that the movement, itself, was racist. He believed the movement divided all Americans. He claimed it had the ability to categorize and judge as racist good people who were otherwise self-possessed or free from racist agitation. Giuliani also waged a popular argument in backlash politics. He claimed that Black Lives Matter cared about Black lives only when Black lives were taken by a White person. He furthered his argument by pointing out its members never protested whenever people were killed in Chicago and, probably, by a Black person.

Contrarily, their criticism exposed the truth behind colorblindness. In fact, the catchphrase was used as another way to change the narrative. Along with the rhetorical hash tag All Lives Matter, it was an admission that White people were more than willing to see skin color as problematic when assigning blame to Black people. More importantly, their criticism obscured the movement's critique of violence, inequality, and injustice found in the legal system.

Donald Trump became known for political posturing on the campaign trail (2015). A pretentious, self-important person, Trump claimed he had all of the answers to America's social problems. While campaigning, he promised to issue an executive order if elected president—one making the death penalty mandatory for anyone who killed a police officer. What a pretentious parade of hard words!

Did it even matter that he had no previous knowledge of politics? Trump was unaware of the compelling acceptance his statement would have on his audience. No US president had that level of authority. But that did not matter. Trump wanted to provoke a political response. And he did, from an otherwise untapped crowd of frustrated voters.

Black Lives Matter became a scapegoat for violence against law enforcement. Conservatives blamed the movement for the recent homicides of law enforcement officers. These homicides were said to be committed by Black people who wanted vengeance against White police abuse of authority. Said to be ambush murders, three particular homicides took place in Brooklyn, New York, Baton Rouge, Louisiana, and Dallas, Texas, between the years 2014 and 2016. Due to the amount of attention received, police homicides became a central theme of the 2016 Republican National Convention (RNC).

Milwaukee Sheriff David Clarke was the first person to speak at the RNC. In a conspicuous attempt to impress his constituents, Clarke began his speech by denouncing Black Lives Matter. He felt the movement was responsible for a breakdown in social complexity. In response to his opening statement, Blue Lives Matter, a new movement was created as an object of fantasy.

Second to speak at the RNC was Rudy Giuliani. He opened a discussion about his concerns for America's wellness. He said many Americans no longer felt safe in their own homes. He also asked for a show of support for police officers who many people felt were being targeted, he claimed.

Miranda Devine, an Australian media personality, also blamed Black Lives Matter. She argued that the killing of an unarmed Australian woman in Minnesota and by a Black police officer was a tragic mistake. She claimed law enforcement officers were under considerable pressure to stay alive due to a war on police. She supported her argument by claiming Black Lives Matter incited a surge of violent activity against law enforcement. The entire movement was built on a lie, she exclaimed. She also purported that Black people were far more likely to kill cops than cops were to kill Black people, a groundless argument offering no supporting evidence.

It is sad to say that when America's social system begins to regress, it's a bad sign for the country's future. All Lives Matter and Blue Lives Matter campaigns were attempts to bring safety and wellness to American communities. Both provided resources that had long-term solutions for preserving American customs, traditions, and institutions.

However, as antagonistic reactions to Black Lives Matter, each created unrealistic depictions of Black

Americans. In that way, both camps were persuaded by the unbending, pitiless resistance of conservatism. Their reactions to existing members of America—Blacks, Latinos, Native Americans (American Indians), females, people of different cultures, individuals from low socioeconomic backgrounds, immigrant families, political refugees, and other minorities—impacted profoundly on many communities.

The problem was both camps, either intentionally or unintentionally, supported a system of discriminatory policies that promoted racial inequality and social injustice. In the end, many communities were better off than either camp could achieve, united.

Events that unfolded between the years 2014 to 2016 most likely worked to undermine public trust in the Democratic process. And with the 2016 US presidential election taking place, people were separated by substantially different political ideologies. Those who followed Bernie Sanders, people who viewed the gradually changing face of America as regressive. Bernie lost in the primaries, but continued to build momentum after his campaign.

Trump supporters, who appeared to be happy and waiting for the return of America's discriminatory past. And supporters of Hillary Clinton who supported several of her political themes to include expanding women's rights, instituting campaign finance reform, raising middle-class income, and improving the Affordable Care Act. Along with Russian spy networks or so-called troll farms aimed at destabilizing the country, it pointed to a political situation that could have erupted into a civil war.

There were only four times in US history where the Electoral College voted against the people's choice or the popular vote. Hillary Rodham Clinton became the fifth presidential nominee to win the popular vote but lose the election. How did it happen? Government officials were convinced Russia interfered in the 2016 election.

The operation was ordered by Russian President, Vladimir Putin. Its purpose was to interfere in the 2016 US presidential election. Its goal was to assist Donald Trump in winning the US Presidency. The operation was carried out to weaken public trust in the Democratic process.

It was also designed to ruin Hillary Clinton's creditability, electability and, ultimately, end her chances of winning the US presidency. All activity of Putin's interference was confirmed by the United States intelligence community in October of 2016.

The problem with Russia's interference was one of possible collusion. Collusion was said to have occurred between members of the Trump campaign and Russia. The intelligence community reported that Vladimir Putin assisted the Trump campaign in winning the US election.

The US intelligence report was said to be saturated with an enormous amount of evidence, linking the Trump Campaign. But what possible intentions did Russia have with interfering in the US presidency? Russia's intentions concerning US elections were to use cyber tools and media campaigns to sway US public opinion.

The Federal Bureau of Investigation (FBI), National Security Agency (NSA), and Central Intelligence Agency (CIA) all endorsed the report. A Trump appointed government official, Director of Intelligence Dan Coats, supported the findings of other agencies after the Helsinki summit. Report findings, Trump strongly ignored.

Trump repeatedly denied accusations that President Putin assisted him in winning the election. However, the report claimed Putin assisted Trump by speaking favorably about him and discrediting Hillary Clinton, publically and on social media. Trump countered accusations against him by insisting Putin attempted to help Clinton win the election, not him.

Trump also claimed Putin did not favor him in the 2016 election. And, why not: Trump said he had ambitions of advancing the US military and increasing US energy production; and, that would hurt Russia, he exclaimed. But, at the Helsinki summit, Putin said since Trump talked favorably about stabilizing US Russia relations, he wanted Trump to win.

According to the US intelligence report, major political parties were targeted by Russian intelligence services. Operations were said to focus on associated targets of the US presidential election. The report did conclude Russia collected data on the Republican Party, but failed to conduct a comparable analysis against associated targets.

Trump repeatedly denied Russia's attempt at hacking Republican computer servers. But, he did say the

Democratic Party was severely compromised due to a lack of security. In any event, Trump vehemently denied collusion with Russia.

Cyberattacks against the Democratic National Convention (DNC) were reported. Russia gained access to the Democratic National Committee network in July of 2015. Its spies maintained access until at least June of 2016.

Russia collected data on the US primaries, think tanks, and lobbying groups capable of instigating change in public policy. Trump continued to deny collusion, citing the possibility of involvement from communist countries like China, North Korea, et cetera. The Democratic Party suffered a tremendous lost as hundreds of classified emails surfaced belonging to Hillary Clinton.

Russia's campaign against Hillary Clinton included intelligence agencies that conducted covert operations, like cyber activity, with a combined messaging strategy carry out by government agencies, state-funded media, intermediaries, contract social media users or trolls, and disciplinarians such as the Internet Research Agency of Professional Trolls.

Located in Saint Petersburg, Russia, its members were in close allegiance with Putin. Trolls were paid to propagate myths about Hillary Clinton. They also spread false information to perpetuate half truths about Clinton and the Clinton campaign. Months after tech giants released ads showing how trolls undermine public trust, thirteen Russian agents and 3 Russian business firms were indicted on federal charges for their involvement.

President Trump insisted that the Russia collusion investigation turned up no evidence of criminal wrongdoing between his 2016 presidential campaign and Russia. And after two years of investigating, on March 24, 2019, US Attorney General William P. Barr released to the public an investigation summary called the Mueller Report.

Special Counsel Robert Mueller, in his much anticipated report, concluded there was no collusion between the Trump campaign and communist Russia. Mueller, a former Director of the Federal Bureau of Investigation (2013), exonerated President Donald J. Trump on charges of colluding with Russia. The report also concluded that there was not enough evidence to pursue charges against President Trump on interfering in the Russia Trump investigation.

Throughout its intellectual history, America suffered a series of strife between both Democratic and Republican Parties. Minorities continued to face widespread discrimination in housing, education, and employment as well as taunting in their own homeland against their religious rights.

Democrats and Republicans continued to insult and demoralize each other well into the new millennium. Republican supporters continued to encourage reactionary behaviors in minorities who opposed their party's attempts to gain control of the executive, legislative, and judicial branches and, ultimately, the country. It also showed that when people's needs go unmet, the country will suffer strife or discord.

Chapter 7
Black Morality: A Taboo Topic among White Americans

People ought to understand that we were not fighting for the right to integrate; we were fighting against white supremacy.

Stokely Carmichael (1941-1998)

People living in Western cultures, like North America, are obsessed with equality and yet fear change. This obsession comes from conservative Whites having an unhealthy preoccupation with developing a utopian society. Having to set the highest values possible in order to achieve their goal ultimately means dim hopes for a utopian future. In this thesis, such desires are rooted in visceral feelings about having to cope with perceived differences in Black morality, a taboo topic among conservative White Americans. The hope, here, is an opened dialogue will take place within and between these two cultural systems.

Dominant myth portray conservatives as concerned with the ultimate perfectibility of man, that is, being the best possible. Such utopian beliefs cause people to set excessively high moral or intellectual values in a society that functions under impossibly ideal conditions. In addition to the utopian myth, that of an idealized morality, their myths portray White folk as a people who work to alleviate suffering. It also shows consideration in ways that associates their race with a divine power. There are Christian Whites (having the divine capacity for love) and atheist Whites (disbelievers of religion who are only concerned with ethical and moral principles). Then there are conservative Whites (advocating the best in society and opposing radical changes). Conservative ideology pertains

197

directly to or resembles, most closely, White utopian values.

Finally, there are liberal Whites who are idealistic social reformers. Liberals claim to be more concerned with progress, reform, and the protection of civil liberties. Conservatives brand these broad-minded individuals troublemakers for their views on what constitutes utopia. Each utopian portrayal recognizes White people in a distorted, yet humanizing imagery said to distinguish them from minorities whose natural abilities are considered to function beneath the collar of Whites.

For White Americans, the paradox of Black morality is one where in open spaces they are no longer concerned with distinctions between Blacks and themselves. Yet behind closed doors, the mere idea of Black influence on White culture is largely unacceptable, associated with profound pessimism. We all know Black morality is largely a taboo topic in America. Hell, this concept started during the indentured servitude of Blacks when former apprentices became popular among English speaking females. Yet, most people fail to consider the social implications of perpetuating myths about Black morality and how it impacts our perceptions.

During the civil rights movement, the threat of racial integration terrorized many Whites. Integration terrorized those who were fearful about Black morality or myths of their immorality. For Black people, the movement was primarily about establishing equal and greater opportunities to succeed in a nation considered hostile.

Their history, up to that point in time, was primarily about social exclusion and persecution of Black people who were considered unacceptable. The integration of Blacks into mainstream society, a concept never fully realized, continues to bring forth more questions about Black morality. Yet, mimicking African American athletes and public figures, increasingly common among young White children today, reflects idealistic patterns that, in many ways, show a willingness to embrace change.

Humane interaction, often shown by Whites in the coming generation, laid the groundwork for progress, reform, and liberal racial attitudes today. In the 1980's and 1990's, listening and dancing to the abrasive lyrics of hip hop legends like LL Cool J., NWA, and Wu Tang Clan raised social awareness and increased cultural literacy for many White youth. Such cultural development deepened the conscious minds of Americans on the home front. Along with the profound mixture of music from popular culture, mainstream culture had to change their contemporary attitudes about minorities living in America.

In fact, the reason why Newt Gingrich had to bow out of the political campaign for presidency early in 2012 was because of his inability to code racist language in a way that reflected everyday decorum. The classic rhetoric of Senator Mitt Romney, segregationist and longtime critic of interracial relationships as well as same-sex marriages, showed how change in the social climate could affect even a political reactionist. Romney was also a member of the

199

Mormon Church where his principles continue to be accepted and protected in "the bosom of the family."

Conservative Whites continue to view segregation as part of a wholesome American value system. Due to their segregationist beliefs, there are still many conservative supporters who have wrongful impressions of Black people. As a result, the exaggeratedly proper attitudes displayed by Whites cease slowly. Along with their limited understanding of minorities, they often show a willful disobedience to or disrespect for people who endorse racial integration.

Ironically, Whites in the coming generation show a much more accepting attitude toward racial integration today. Attitudes show much more positivity than before, even if myths persist. This humanity is a curious progression not to be celebrated or rejoiced, but cautiously approached. What looks like genuine change in racial attitudes may be more of a growing curiosity about Black people. Although music has a universal appeal, portrayal of young Blacks as gangster rappers and video vixens threaten to continue the challenge of humane interaction in which relationships are marked out or motivated by concern. In fact, what we have here is a property-owning class who may be more interested in propagating myths of Black immorality, rather than strengthening the truth about their morality.

Strengthening Black morality is critical. Why? Much of the myth about White attitudes and behaviors feed back into Black contempt or self-hatred. Since Blacks refuse, on many levels, to love themselves, especially the norm of beauty, like their matted hair, wide noses, full lips, and big hips causes them to defeat their own ambitions in life. Self-defeating thoughts, self-abuse, self-betrayal, and self-fulfilling prophecy are social anxiety disorders that disturb Black people in the same way as other racial and cultural groups.

The same way Whites show contempt for Black morality, Black people display open disrespect for themselves and, often at times, due to very different reasons. In fact, all one needs to do is degrade their natural abilities in a way that causes them anxiety and they will develop self-defeating thoughts. The degradation of a cultural group will bring shame to them in ways that what comes next is fear.

Fear is sustained by convincing Black people they are intellectually underdeveloped and less civilized. Thus, their people warrant less concern than strangers and others. The oppression of slavery and the system of segregation that followed it are part of that reasoning. In contrast, such supremacy practices all but failed due to the creative efforts of past and present White and Black activists. People like Pearl S. Buck, Morris Dees, US Representative John Lewis, Harry Belafonta, and a laundry list of others campaigned and continue to campaign for racial equality and social justice in America.

Yet, to deprive a people of self-concept and esteem ultimately affects how the human psyche will respond during humane interaction. It may very well be that Black morality or their perceived immorality has, primarily, a motivative function. The arousal of such functions clearly compels people to behave in characteristic ways.

How do people learn to consider Blacks if Whites have contempt for them? Why do Whites fear Black morality? Can change bring about humane interaction for Black people living in a society that openly disrespects them? The hope is to shed light on these questions by establishing truth about Black humanity in social spaces that affirm White contempt, especially situations where minorities adopt the social roles of their oppressors.

People have to face the harsh reality that Blacks and other minorities often take on the social roles of their oppressors. Why are minorities so accommodating? Whites put a premium on their lifestyles. Mainstream living requires cultural groups to accept suffering while each accommodates White people in exploitative and oppressive ways. In this way, accommodation will prevent minorities from changing the prevailing current of thought.

It also keeps racial and cultural minorities from developing activities aimed at bringing about an overthrow to oppressive governments. Only minorities who are considered to be model citizens will benefit from the acculturative pressures of change, especially individuals who relinquish their cultural identity to move into the larger society. In this way, minorities would have to make an agreement with dominant Whites. That being said, if Blacks are to have any chance of benefitting from mainstream culture, they will have to abandon their principles.

Abandoning one's moral principles is viewed by many to be a form of selling out. It involves assimilating new ideas into an existing school of thought. Minorities may be absorbed into an established mainstream or merge to form a new society. Assimilation encourages learning that takes place as a daily process of cultural development. It teaches racial and cultural minorities not to be subversive and transgressive, be it through communism, authoritarianism, or American capitalism.

Yet, have we not learned anything from the tragicomic events of Michael Steele. His reality was turned upside down due to this realization. Assimilation gives cultural groups good reason to set expectations high, usually by exhorting members to become more American (in Steels case, Whiter). Since life in the cultural mainstream was considered superior for so many years, assimilating minorities was thought to be best for American society. Although there are those who continue to support assimilation, more people support other, healthier adaptations to acculturation. It can also be stressful due to feelings of alienation and identity loss in which there may be no selective involvement between two cultural systems to provide a supportive base for effective coping. In short, minorities lose important credibility with smaller, less dominant cultural groups when they assimilate their ideals into the larger, more dominant society.

Yet, other minorities in the United States will find continuous contact with mainstream society stressful. Contact with Whites often causes discordance between legitimate expectations and present actualities. How is social discord possible? Thanks to modern progress and social reform, minorities and their families enjoy greater material comfort. They also enjoy more political freedom than in past times. In spite of that, when comparing themselves to the cultural mainstream, many develop feelings of depravity. Why so? Although living standards have improved, new conditions exist below normative expectations compared to dominant Whites.

Once the reality of their situation dawns on them, many minorities will adjust to acculturative pressures. These adjustments mean, in many instances, minorities will provide their lives to better accommodate the scheme of White production. The hope is, in return for cooperation within the larger social system, they will be given greater material comfort and more political freedom than in previous times. Perhaps they will even gain greater selective involvement from mainstream culture.

Again, in this way, acceptance means only model minorities will benefit. Incidentally, Whites have for years obsessively condemned circumstances where Black morality is concerned. They have deprived Black Americans of earning a decent living income, better housing is still a considerable problem, then there's healthcare and educational opportunities, all work to deprive them in ways we would not expect people to live.

White people fear Black morality. Their fear also brings them anxiety. This vague unpleasant emotion is due to experiences White people acquired from trying to enslave or dispossess Blacks, world cultures even. Having anxiety also imply White people fear the same exclusionary policy of racial inequality they imposed on minorities throughout their intellectual history. But, for them to acknowledge their anxious or apprehensive feelings, even as they continue to instill fear in Black people, is an admission of guilt or weakness. A few politicians, historians, and researchers have since acknowledged Whites have hidden Black people's natural history in fear of negative consequences. That educating Blacks is the most perceived source of fear among conservative Whites does not sway Black determination, however.

Black determination is taboo among conservative White Americans. It is a motivation they often try to possess but, over which, have no controlling influence. In this way, it often arouses a glandular aversion to materialistic changes in values, be it an obsession with new development in the social environment, or blatant contempt for Black progress.

On one hand, Black determination includes Afrocentricity of which there is no room for White influence. In this way, Blacks only reference Whites to accentuate their own history. Afrocentrists ask the philosophical question, "What would Black people do if there were no White people in the World?" Afrocentrists answer this question by asserting the central role of Black people within a cultural context of African history, thereby removing Whites from the center of Black reality.

This Afrocentric form of Black morality is based on the notion all people who descend from Africa should act or intervene on people's inhumanity to cure their own insanity. This assertion can be quite problematic for conservative Whites who deny their misgivings and wrongdoings to the detriment of other cultures (as in American slavery and South African apartheid, for example).

On the other hand, Black determination in America is, today, based on needs that go unmet and over which there appears to be no legal precedence established to support its urgency. In fact, the dominant myth among White women and men is that Blacks contribute to their own plight by lacking in ambition and failing to take advantage of opportunities. For instance, they often fail to complete high school, have poor work ethics, and undeveloped social skills, which fails to highlight the strength of Black determination. The lack of work ethics and cultural values allow for Whites to remain passive. Their passiveness, however, is hardly an acceptable response for a nation considered powerful enough to influence events throughout the world.

Certainly, Whites have no real understanding of how Black determination is supposed to work, only positive and negative outcomes involving what actually takes place. In this way, their discomfort is influenced by the dominant myth Black people are expected to become or be, in prospect, a threat to White utopian values. Relationships between these two cultural systems span out in ways that reveal the real potential of Black people. This notion leads to the uneasiness of Whites who, in turn, socially exclude Black people from opportunities. Their refusal to consider Black possibility is also an embarrassment, derived from shameful feelings Black people are critically aware of wrongdoings against them.

In addition, the inability to rest their concerns lead to a fear Blacks have some untapped potential that can influence change in various dimensions of culture. It is fear among conservatives that causes many to silence talk about Black morality, making it a taboo topic among White Americans. On the face of it all, White discomfort, uneasiness, and fear gives an edge to Black people, assuming the dominant myth about their immorality is real.

There is a more sinister way of looking at it, however. If Black morality shows a people whose determination has the potential to influence change, then are not Blacks worthy of White consideration? One of the key assumptions White people have about Blacks is their principles are not right, moral, or just. Yet, when Black people view themselves as centered on and central to their own history, they become productive members of society rather than marginal, not burdening the responsibility of already overburdened and unresponsive bureaucratic systems. Using that sociocultural paradigm, researchers discovered interaction is based on attitudes and behaviors we can predict.

Further, it is understood that as interaction develops cognition increases to the extent we can appreciate people who like the same things and share similar attitudes. Well then, what similarities exist between these two cultural systems that would make members of mainstream culture want to include Black people into the mainstay of American life? There are many cultural similarities. But, to concentrate on similarities found in one group often causes the relative exclusion of others.

Do you remember Present Ronald W. Reagan? When he ran for reelection, Reagan made a pitch for the Hispanic vote. Do you remember that? Many Blacks looked at the abrupt move with disdain. Other Blacks felt alienated and betrayed. Why so, do you ask? Reagan promised to aid Hispanics in maintaining their cultural integrity while helping them to become an integral part of the larger society.

However, the prevailing current of thought focused on problems that persisted for Black Americans. Once Republicans began to concentrate their efforts on integrating Hispanics, Black people understood America would renege on a longtime promise to help them reach full equality. Needless to say, Reagan won the popular vote among Hispanics, taking 49 states on his way to reelection. Many acculturating Hispanics would soon turn in their second-class status to become part of the career oriented, professional class. Blacks, on the other hand, would be met with strong resistance in ways that continue to impede their ability to achieve.

Republicans have since reinstituted their campaign against social programs, like affirmative action and school desegregation. Many Blacks have come to develop feelings of inferiority in that way. A few more relinquished their cultural identity only to join Republicans and their Post-Party Conservative movement. As a result of these incidences, Black Americans continue to have difficulty achieving equality and more than any group in American society.

How can Blacks learn to cope with adversity? How can Black morality work to liberate a people from racism and racial discrimination? Such a system of oppression reinforces dominant myths or condemns Black people to suffering while they learn to see their own morality as taboo. There are indeed many ways to cope. And, through the adversity of it all, Black people continue to show remarkable resilience and adaptation. Yet, racial tensions and prejudice often occur between these two cultural systems whenever Black people attempt to move forward toward progress and reform.

The situation worsens for Black women, many of whom face overwhelming adversity. In fact, Black women are the poorest cultural group in America. Yet, there can be no movement forward for Black men without the help and influence of Black women. In this way, the exclusion of Black women is inexcusable and without justification.

Black male morality differs from Black female morality in terms of their undifferentiated consciousness. Black females tend to internalize their self-concept and esteem. In this way, their morality becomes vested in soulful expressions of spirituality over which there is a struggle between good and evil.

Men, on the other hand, externalize this mental attitude into principles of right or wrong. In their way, Black men fight for breath to survive in the patriarchal structure of dominant White society. Dominant myth about Black male morality depicts them as being obsessed with violent social behavior. After all, crime in the United States is blamed on Black males and their perceived inabilities rather than White resistance and the feminization of poverty, though attitudes are slowly changing.

In addition, Black men are blamed for criminal behavior we see among mainstream American youth today. Curiously, Black influence has much to do with White children imitating and mimicking Black styles and mannerisms. Clothing, their manner of walking, and mental attitudes displayed through communication styles, readily reflect "the Afro-Americanization of White youth" as Dr. Cornel West says. In this way, we see a culture expressing its needs in ways that have gone unmet.

The struggle of Black morality is generally accepted as a spiritual bout between good and evil. Therefore, it is not so much a power struggle based on right and wrong. Why? Good people do bad things for the right reason. Black people understand the time is ripe for great moral changes in society. Many believe it is most suitable or just for dominant White society to recognize the sheer absurdity that confronts Black people living in America today.

Blacks must learn to no longer see themselves through the aesthetic lens of White male supremacy. In addition, so long as they conform to the social standards and cultural expectations used to continuously devalue their people, Blacks will never value themselves.

Michael Jackson, who died from a drug overdose, had romantic notions of successfully assimilating into mainstream culture. He received perms, cosmetic alterations (illegibly), and implants. How come? Some would say he found himself frustrated from wanting something he could not have: acceptance in a world that continuously devalued his Black features. Tragically, Michael Jackson's untimely death served only to reinforce a rather widespread belief of self-hatred found among acculturating persons who move into the larger society.

Augmentation is a moral choice to enhance one's self-image. Such change in one's personal appearance more often results from having a low self-concept and esteem. People believe Michael's frustration, in trying to fit into mainstream culture, was an internal struggle between good and evil. In this way, Michael hoped the good he contributed to society and throughout the world would outweigh, perhaps, bad feelings White people associate with Black morality. In his case, Michael feared becoming a terrible person like his father. Michael, augmenting his physical appearance in concert with adopting White children (which I failed to mention, earlier), was a man who cried out through his music to be **R**espected, **A**pproved, **C**herished, and **E**steemed. Michael's attempt to

211

relinquish his cultural identity reinforces the notion that some Black people do see life through the aesthetic lens of White male supremacy.

Is there any wonder why Blacks and other minorities only made historical impressions on Whites as entertainers and athletes? This vicious cycle has come to teach White people many stereotypes about minorities are more of a reality than first imagined. Although minorities are highly competitive, the impression is they can only excel in mindless areas with no concern for consequences that require moral aptitude or human intellect.

Mohamad Ali suffered from a mysterious case of Parkinson's disease moments after his last fight; Florence Griffin Joyner (Flo-Jo) died from steroid overdose; and, Redd Foxx died a womanizer and needlessly in poverty. Many more minority performers would meet with failed attempts at stardom. In this way, unreliable definitions, or generalizations about minorities, become real. So, we label them inferior.

We label them. And why so do you ask? Their attitudes and behaviors are defined according to the misconception of Whites who, again, may be more often interested in exploiting myths of Black immorality, rather than strengthening the truth about their morality. Self-fulfilling prophecy prevents most Whites from seeing the level of potential found among minorities struggling to achieve greatness in mainstream American culture today.

On the other hand, Whites understand all too well the feelings associated with social inadequacy, since most live in a privileged world that involves keeping up with the Joneses: an idiom that refers to comparing specific neighbors to a particular standard of status, wealth, and material possession. Keeping up with the Joneses is driven by feelings of social inadequacy. Failure to keep up with the Joneses is considered by many people to be a sign of social and economical inferiority.

Let's consider the working poor, for instance. Many are full-time workers who depend on public assistance to survive. Then there are rich people like Donald Trump who, at the time, owned the most expensive home in America at a cost of about $250M. Where you are on the social latter can lead to inferior thinking, including envy brought on from seeing the success of others (personified as one of the seven deadly sins).

Feelings of inferiority follows the reasoning minorities are unable to perform important tasks. In contrast, rather than devoting their time to professions such as technician, mason, or scientist, many minorities are forced into inferior positions, often at times, based on cultural stereotypes. Evidently, your status makes a vital difference in how people will perceive you.

Yet, in a capitalist society governed by patriarchy, most Black people do not show spite and resentment at seeing the success of their oppressors. However, such myth continues to explain the worldview of Black people. The problem Black people face with morality in today's society often manifests through chronic living conditions. Inadequate housing, dangerous neighborhoods, burdensome

213

responsibilities, and economic uncertainties create negative perceptions, and all at the hands of already overburdened and unresponsive bureaucratic systems.

However, this situation is seriously grim for Black women who Whites fear less than Black men. Morality for Black women is not defined as unimportant because they are morally obligated to the Black man. But since Black women are viewed as more marginal in American culture. This notion comes from the Black woman's inability to provide financial support for her family throughout history. Unfortunately, her social situation does not improve much in the Black community.

For instance, while Black women can express their own needs, they're not often given status and power in their community. Moreover, many are despised today. Why is that statement true? They seek independent careers and sometimes replace Black men in society as the head of household. In addition to bringing relief to a dire financial situation, Black women are devalued and unappreciated both in White and Black domains. They are also the poorest members of any cultural group in the United States.

Sexual imagery also plays a well known role in reinforcing the dominant myth about Black morality. Black males are type cast as sexual predators by conservative Whites who become intimidated over their vigorous nature. This justifies oppressing them to the protection of White female innocence. In addition to stereotyping Black men, conservatives assume the morals of Black women are corrupt as the forbidden fruit. They are cast as over sexualized, seductive, promiscuous, and now selfish vixens, women without conscious, having an insatiable desire for wealth, and guilt behind them. In that way, the dominant myth of Black morality is marked by immorality and perversion.

Still, there is a grimmer reality about Black female morality, a world in which they endure greater stigmatization. White women always thought of Black females as Mammy, a wholesome, yet unattractive and morbidly obese woman in worn cloths. She was supposed to have a strong superstitious and spiritual belief that opposed conventional wisdom. White women use to recognize her as the maid who took care of the White man's home and children. But her most important quality was she always humbled in the present of "White authority." The White man's relationship with Mammy was said to develop from that moral sense of reasoning. However, his motives further disturbed gender equality to a twist that can also explain cultural problems we attribute to sexism and sexual discrimination.

White men stereotyped Mammy as socially dominant and more competent compared to Black men. White men claimed she could be relied upon to support and comfort others far beyond the reaching point, breaking cultural expectations. Their claims intimidated White women who traditionally associated the trait with Black men.

Instead of Mammy being undesirable, as most White women assumed, she was kept by White men as someone pleasurable and worth their consideration. In this way, the strength of Black women further justified the White man's sexual indiscretions, a state of infidelity come to be known as "The Great Social Evil." This downgraded experience offended White women's sensibilities. The relationship between their husbands and the Black woman whom they owned would soon raise concerns. George Washington and Thomas Jefferson both married into wealth. As evident, they found it desirable to have sexual relations with Black women, concubines of slavery, who were considerably younger and seemingly healthier.

Today, Whites continue to show disgust for DNA evidence corroborating the age-old rumor Thomas Jefferson had sexual relations with a Black slave whose name is well known today: Sally Hemings, his concubine. Whites are also in denial about Venus, a slave who mothered most of George Washington's children, and one of two concubines brought into servitude by him. In fact, the idea that Black children are born lighter in hue is greatly accepted as a terrible consequence of slavery.

Victorian styles of fashion are also seen as an admission about a people whose physical features are perceived to be more intriguing and interesting. Noted for elegantly lavish gowns—trimmed metal hoop skirts worsened by tight corsets, under-pointed with boned bodices of whalebone and steel, which gave White women the illusion of sexual endowment—Victorian clothing added legitimacy to "The Great Social Evil."

In fact, Victorian fashion strongly supported claims that White men were sexually attracted to Black women. As for the cultural-based gender stereotype about Black women (that of a sexually unrestrained woman), they were then and still are the object of White men's sexual desires. Yet, White women and their ideals of beauty, as Dr. Cornel West puts it:

> ...put a premium on lightness and womanhood in ways that undermines the nature of rich feminine styles associated with Black women.

Today, Black people are viewed as disgusting, dirty, or common. These cultural stereotypes perpetuate the myth by which White people continue to view them. Misconceptions not only reinforce negative stereotypes about Blacks, but in the case of interaction, arouse disgust and aversion in people, many of whom consider them less acceptable. This social distinction defiles Black people in ways that deprive them of their cultural identity.

Consequently, the contributions to breaking up Black families cause an insufficient balance in intergroup relations. And such imbalance creates poverty, which further justifies the sexual indiscretions of White men. Some historians believe the suffering and loss of self-respect imposed on Black Americans extended the limitation of exploration for writers and artists eager to uncover myths about Black erotica. Many were fearful they would establish a reality or correctness, reinforcing the dominant myth. In this way, stereotypes bring an end to any personal concerns people may have as a genuine sign of interest.

So long as Black morality remains a taboo topic, we cannot begin to describe the thoughts, feelings, and motives that characterize each one of us. Hence, we must unravel the myth! Such an unraveling brings legitimacy to a problem that deserves considerable attention. It's within our best interests to determine whether the myth about Black morality is central to or minimal in the daily lives of everyday, ordinary people.

Resolution means any and every research investigation conducted must involve the concrete realities of lived experiences, thus making sociocultural influences a key component in understanding Black morality. Our refusal limits any possibility to confront the overwhelming realities of racism and racial discrimination. Only when Black people raise their self-concept and esteem, will conservative Whites stop associating spiritual or soulful matters found in Black communities with perversion. It is only through their undifferentiated consciousness can such change take place. This form of progression is requisite for healthy intergroup relationships. Why so? It's not because White and Black people should live separate and equal lives. But, since what troubles America in the first place is her natural discomfort, uneasiness, and inherent fear of Black people.

In discussing taboo topics like Black morality, we also reduce visceral feelings that strengthen it. If, however, we fail to ascertain the vast ways by which Black people act humanely, our ignorance will render us concerned only with myths of their immorality.

In examining Black morality, we uncover cultural problems society chooses to ignore. Recognizing Black people, or their ethical and moral principles, is not by any means a way to introduce radical changes in society or subvert the political views of conservatives and their warped priorities. Failure to recognize Black morality proves even highly developed Western cultures, like America, can be obsessed with equality at the same time it fears change. Such information should be integrated into Western logic rather than ignored at the risk of alienating minorities, world cultures even.

Epilogue
Diversity and Divergence

The new millennium is an exciting era for us as Americans. We've witnessed the election of our first ever African American President. He led the country, brilliantly, during his first term even in what seemed to be insurmountable odds stacked up against him. Conservatives and Republicans are engaged in lively debate about whether they will continue to move forward toward liberal racial attitudes or resist further change. The economy is doing better. And, violence by Whites toward Blacks is getting attention.

Yet, diversity threatens to widen the cultural divide. In fact, it promises to be one of the most challenging topics in America, for years to come even. Why? Diversity drives at the very core of American democracy. It will force us to take a realistic look at modern progress and social reform. In essence, diversity enables us to take a closer look at cultural problems that affect the circumstances of everyday, ordinary people.

In the past, Whites thought of diversity as people from different Europeans nations coming together to form a homogeneous melting pot. That was then. Today, as America grows more diverse, Whites worry about the level of destructive conflict and violence becoming increasingly common. There is heightening concern that immigrant families, political refugees, and other minorities will become the next state of rebellious dissatisfaction for White people in the country.

The Boston Marathon bombing of 2013, conducted by Bosnian immigrants Dzhokhar and Tamerlan Tsarnaev, gives America cause for concern. The influx of Africans, Latinos, Asians, and other minority groups also increase concerns. Due to their discomfort, uneasiness, and inherent fear, many Whites want immigrants to be teased apart from the mainstay of dominant White society rather than have them live in concert.

There are too few institutions through which one can experience the entire feel of American diversity. Grade school, college, and other institutions fall grossly short in helping people gain this experience. However, gone are the days when minorities compete for White peer approval! Precedence must now be given to the relative power and status of minority groups involved. Why? Many show remarkable resilience and adaptation by building their own communities and social structures.

They develop social structures that help them adapt to life in America. They have Black churches, Japanese language schools, Mexican American kin systems, Jewish colleges and, along with developing highly impressive strategies to help buffer the effects of severe stress and oppression, have adapted coping mechanisms to help them survive in the face of overwhelming adversity. Despite the fact White America has, on occasion, tried to enslave or dispossess Black Americans, world cultures even, the vast majority continue to negotiate with its adherents. Although they have essentially mastered two cultures, racial tensions and hostility emerge when minorities attempt to move into historically White communities.

As minorities attempt to penetrate historically White communities, interracial tensions mount. In this way, minorities have difficulty reaching equality. And though the vast majority of Whites appear to show support for minorities than just a few decades earlier, occasional incidents still spark tensions and prejudice between these cultural systems.

There is also strong resistance shown by conservatives to supporting programs like Affirmative Action and school desegregation, political programs designed to help minorities achieve. As a result, White Americans, particularly conservatives in White leadership, resist the upward mobility of minorities. Here, they play the old racial card to maintain control of our political system. Such resistance enables them to displace blame on Black people for continued problems allowed to build decades earlier.

Displacing blame causes divergence. Whites claim the problem begins when minorities, like Black Americans, fail to consider opportunities. They claim Blacks will not take advantage of opportunities other minorities are simply willing to consider. However, their observations often follow inexperience in which case Whites draw inappropriate attention to Blacks by making vulgar remarks about them. Their nasty comments combined with proud, self-serving remarks more often leads them to legitimize discrimination against Black people. Even when Blacks attempt to seek out their fair share in housing, education, and employment markets, Whites continue to discriminate.

Once racial tensions and hostility emerge, requiring a resolution, as it often does, they dismiss the minority viewpoint, and cultural relations destabilize.

Curiously, there is a growing trend for minorities not to improve themselves in intergroup relations. They have begun to form their own communities and social structures with people who hold certain attitudes and interests in common. They are demanding that America respects their decision not to assimilate. Paired with the density of racial heritage found forty years prior, diversity is even more complex than just a decade earlier.

They also insist their new government accommodates their personal needs to achieve a stable, sustainable culture within the social contexts of dominant White influence. This position often means reestablishing ties to their former nation or accrediting minority success to the doctrines of their former country. Along with existing prejudices, for instance, Croatians are at war with Bosnian Muslims, and Israeli denigration of Palestinians. The Japanese display prejudice toward Chinese who continue to show hostility for Tibetans. East Indians have learned to look down on all those who are not of equal religious standing. White Americans tend to strongly dislike all nationalities. And, everyone seems to dislike the nihilistic thinking strategies of African Americans. The congestion from various nationalities mixed into one big melting pot of preexisting identities, some would say, contributes to conservatism and discomfort, uneasiness, and fear of change.

Diversity is no doubt an increasing concern for Americans. However, a bigger problem for us to remember is that there exists greater diversity within one racial or ethnic group, than between two or more. The notion of a melting pot of cultures: White American, Black American, Hispanic American, Native American, Asian American, Italian American, German American, and so on, means people will categorized one another into homogeneous groups. How come? Such information is too much for us to process at one time. What's important for us to remember is that no one group shares every characteristic in common and that such descriptions are uncommon across all groups.

Hispanic Americans are the most diverse ethnic group in America. Although many Hispanics are Catholic, others have different religious upbringing. Historically, Hispanics were comprised of Mexicans. But today, they are among the many who come from Central and South American countries, or with Spanish backgrounds.

Before Christopher Columbus, there were 25,000 Native American groups in the United States. Today, they are still a complicated racial group, with Hispanics making up an even greater composite of ethnic variations. Native Americans are now a distinct racial group. But, once upon a time, they too were variations of Asians. Although Native Americans still share in genetic heritage with Asians, among and between these groups, there is still considerable diversity and individual variation.

If you cannot tell by now, diversity and divergence involves complex turns to negotiate. Often, minorities are victimized because of their diversity. Not only do minorities suffer from social injustice, more importantly, their identity is shaped and colored by discomfort, uneasiness, and fear. Consequently, while most minorities are not threatened by their ascribed identity, they work hard to reprove misconceptions or misunderstandings of what social roles they and their children might rightfully play in society.

In contrast, we rarely have leaders who underscore the importance of cultural unity, encourage greater equality, or promote multiculturalism as a process of American democracy. Instead, what dominant Whites put forth is conforming to the standards and conventions of middle-class White America. Such a bourgeois ideology of self-preservation reflects xenophobic resentment toward minorities living in America.

In sum, American society is increasing in diversity. Diversity involves understanding how well White Americans receive minorities. Although many people are well-meaning, those who do understand diversity can teach us a lot about how divergence affects a minority's self-concept. To allow cultural groups to exist as citizens, but disregard their beliefs and opinions as unessential to the American infrastructure, is unjust.

For minorities, people who often believe in social reform, such discrimination shapes the context of their daily lives. Yet, even for minorities, diversity continues to create divergence. Since diversity appears to bring forth discomfort, uneasiness, and fear of change, the adoption of conservatism is an irony.

Need I remind the reader what we understand today about each other is based on White, middle-class cultural bias. If we, as a nation, are to move beyond Western culture's intellectual limitations, Americans better find out what is important and beneficial for people living life in a diverse and increasingly multicultural society.

REFERENCES

Alexander, M. (2015). Facebook [On-line]
  Available:
  https://www.facebook.com/pages/Michelle-
  Alexander/168304409924191

Barlow, D. H. & Durand, V. M. (2005). Abnormal
  psychology: An integrative approach. Thomas
  Learning™

Bradley, M. (1978). The iceman inheritance: Prehistoric
  sources of western man's racism, sexism and
  aggression. New York, NY: Kayode Publications
  LTD

Comer, R. J. (1996). Fundamentals of abnormal
  psychology. New York: H. W. Freeman and
  Company

Davision, G. C. & Neale, D. (1994). Abnormal psychology.
  (6th ed.) New York: John Wiley & Sons, Inc.

Jones, J. M. (1996). Prejudice and racism. (2nd ed.)
  Columbus OH: McGraw-Hill

Khanna, N. and Johnson, C. (2010). Passing as black: How
  biracial Americans choose identity. Time.com. [On-
  line]. Available:
  http://healthland.time.com/2010/12/16/passing-as-
  black-how-biracial-americans-choose-identity/

Nittle, N. K. (2014). Raising biracial children to be well adjusted. <u>About.com</u>. [On-line] Available: http://racerelations.about.com/od/raceconsciousparenting/a/ RaisingBiracialChildrentoBeWellAdjusted.htm

Santrock, J. W. (1996). <u>Adolescence</u>. (6th ed.). Dubuque, IA: Brown & Benchmark

Sears, D. O. (1987). <u>Symbolic racism</u>. In P. Kitz & D. Taylor (Eds.), Towards the elimination of racism: Profile in controversy. New York: Plenum

Smiley, T. & West, C. (2012). <u>The rich and the rest of us</u>. Carlsbad,California: SmilyBooks

YouTube (2019). All Lives Matter. youtube.com [On-line]

Available: https://www.youtube.com/results?search_query=all +lives+matter

YouTube (2019). Blue Lives Matter. youtube.com [On-line] Available: https://www.youtube.com/results?search_query=blu e+lives+matter

YouTube (2019). Black Lives Matter. youtube.com [On-line] Available: https://www.youtube.com/results?search_query=bla ck+lives+matter

YouTube (2019). Donald J. Trump and Collusion.

youtube.com [On-line] Available: https://www.youtube.com/results?search_query=donald+j.+trump+and+collusion

YouTube (2019). Donald Trump and the road to the white house. youtube.com [On-line] Available: https://www.youtube.com/results?search_query=donald+trump+the+road+to+the+white+house+